JESUS: SELF-PORTRAIT BY GOD

DATE DUE

Enda Lyons

Jesus:
Self-portrait by God

PAULIST PRESS
New York and Mahwah, N.J.

232.1
L991j

Originally published in Ireland by Columba Press.

Imprimatur: + Joseph Cassidy, Archbishop of Tuam, October 25, 1993

Library of Congress Cataloging-in-Publication Data

Lyons, Enda, 1933–
Jesus : Self-portrait by God / by Enda Lyons.
    p.   cm.
    Includes bibliographical references and index.
    ISBN 0-8091-3583-3 (alk. paper)
    1. Incarnation. 2. Jesus Christ—Humanity. 3. Hypostatic union. 4. Jesus Christ—Natures.   I. Title.
BT220.L96   1995
232´.1—dc20   95-12265
                                                                          CIP

Published by Paulist Press
997 Macarthur Boulevard, Mahwah, New Jersey 07430

Printed and bound in the United States of America

Acknowledgements

The approach to Jesus of Nazareth which is followed in this book has evolved largely in the course of my work over a number of years with groups in the West of Ireland, particularly in Tuam, Galway, Balla, Claremorris, and Donamon. I am grateful to all who participated in these groups for their courage to stay with the subject and for their many insights. I am grateful to Sr Laura Boyle who contributed much to the formation and nurturing of many of these groups.

I want to thank in particular those who read the manuscript critically, sometimes more than once: my brother Noel, Fr Colm Burke, Fr Eamonn Conway and my brother Albert of my own diocese, Fr Brian Nolan CM of All Hallows College, Dublin, and Fr Eugene Duffy. I am most grateful indeed to these for their painstaking work and for their comments and suggestions. I am deeply indebted to Fr Michael Brennan who, during his years as Director of the Galway Diocesan Centre for Adult Religious Education, could hardly have been more encouraging and accommodating. I am grateful too to my family, especially to Maureen and Margaret, for being always there in a very supportive way, to my friends, especially those in Galway for whom Slánú is a focus.

All quotations from the Bible are from *The Jerusalem Bible* and quotations from Vatican II are from *The Documents of Vatican II*, edited by Walter M Abbott SJ (London, Geoffrey Chapman, 1967).

Contents

For my nephew
HUGH
and his generation and their educators
... that you may believe
that Jesus is the Christ,
the Son of God,
and that believing this
you may have life through his name.

Jn 20:31

In memory of
CYRIL COLLERAN
(1946-1993)
A friend who sowed so many kinds of seeds
and who loved Hugh's generation so much.
Ag Críost an fómhar

Foreword

Like Martha in the gospel story, the Christian churches can be very busy about many things. The fundamental Christian conviction, however, concerns a single momentous event. It concerns that amazing involvement of God in human life which Christians believe has taken place in Jesus of Nazareth. In other words, it concerns 'the Incarnation'. Proclaiming, explaining and celebrating, in life and in liturgy, the great news of this event is, when all is said, the *raison d'être* of the Christian churches. It is precisely this which constitutes their identity, and it is this, and this alone, which distinguishes them from all other groups, institutions, bodies and religions. It is only when we rejoice in this event that we will be able to rejoice in belonging to a Christian church; it is only then that we will be able to say of belonging to a church something like President Mary Robinson, alluding to W.B. Yeats in her inaugural address, said about belonging to Ireland: 'I am of the Church, come dance with me in the church.'

This book has arisen to a large extent out of working with small groups of Christian women and men, mostly in the West of Ireland, as they and I struggled together to make some sense of this fundamental Christian conviction. The aim of the book is to encourage others like these to focus again on this central truth of faith, to help them to understand it better, and, hopefully, to enable them to rejoice in it and to have their faith and their lives rejuvenated by it.

The book is written particularly for people who are wondering if the idea of Incarnation can make any sense at all today, but who are afraid to admit (sometimes even to themselves) their problems regarding it. It is written for those who have not – or rather who think that they have not – a background in theology.

The questions which the book raises – for example: *could Jesus really have been God? if so, could he really have been human? how much did he know? did he know who he was? what is being 'born of a virgin' all about? how literally are we to take what the gospels say about Jesus?, etc.* – are ones which scholars have long been asking and to which they have found some satisfactory answers. They are, however, questions which, in my experience, many other thinking Christians are not, generally speaking, even today encouraged to ask or helped to pursue. They are questions which these need to ask and to pursue if their faith in Jesus is to survive today.

If one were to judge by the table of contents alone, one might easily form the impression that this book is a series of loosely connected essays on Jesus. This is not at all the case. The book is, in fact, a systematic theological treatment of the Incarnation, having a beginning a middle and (in so far as this is possible at all in a book on the Incarnation) an end.

A point which is emphasised very strongly throughout the book, from beginning to end, is the need to think of Jesus as one who is in the first place a human being. Failure to think of Jesus in this way is, it seems to me, the greatest single obstacle encountered by Christians today in their efforts to make sense of the Incarnation and constitutes the greatest single threat to their belief.

While there are notes to each of the chapters of the book, there is no reference to these in the main text. Those interested in notes will, I trust, consult them spontaneously and without being prompted to do so.

3rd, October, 1993
Enda Lyons,
Bermingham,Tuam, Co. Galway.

Introductory

CHAPTER ONE

Thinking about Jesus today

It is my experience that a lot of confusion exists in the minds of Roman Catholics today regarding who – or what – Jesus of Nazareth is believed to be. Is he supposed to be God? Or is he supposed to be a man? Or is he supposed to be both? (It seems to me that many Catholics have settled – wrongly – for looking on him simply as 'God'.) Since Jesus is the one who is central to christianity and to Christian belief, it is, obviously, very desirable that any confusion regarding him which can be removed, should be removed.

I am convinced that there is only one way in which we can hope to remove or even reduce this confusion. As we set out to try to understand Jesus, we need to adopt, quite consciously and deliberately, a very definite attitude of mind: we need to think of Jesus of Nazareth not, first and foremost, as one who is God, 'a divine Person', but, first and foremost, as one who is a *humble human being*. Faith, hopefully, will lead us to appreciate that this human being is the unique Son of God. But we can hope to understand what this faith-conviction means only if we appreciate that it is a conviction about one who is first and foremost a human being – one of ourselves, one like ourselves, subject to all the limitations which necessarily go with being human.

A Small Step?

To adopt such an attitude might seem to be a very small step for us to take. After all, the fact that Jesus was a human being, another human being, a member of the race, a descendant of 'Adam', was the first and most obvious point about him. Interestingly, it was the one fact about him which required no faith at all in those who met him in the flesh. It was, for example, the one thing about him which we could not imagine even his most eager opponents questioning or challenging. That the Jesus they were dealing with was a man of God, they could and did doubt and challenge, but not that he was a fellow human being! The fact of his being human was so obvious to all who knew him during his life that if any of these were to come back today and find someone speaking the way I am speaking now they would be very puzzled indeed. It would be rather like someone who knew and travelled around Ireland with St Patrick in the fifth century coming back today and finding people talking about the need to think of him as a weak, humble, human being. The people who knew both of these men during their lives, were they to come back years later, might be quite surprised to find how subsequent generations spoke about them and visualised them.

But not so small a step?

To begin thinking of Jesus first and foremost as a human being is not at all, however, so simple a step to take. The fact is that we are not those first disciples of Jesus. Unlike them we have never met Jesus in the flesh. We are, rather, heirs to a long tradition of faith about him, in particular about what is known as his 'divinity'. Almost since birth we are accustomed to thinking about him, not so much as a human being, but as 'a divine person'. And it is this great faith-conviction which seems to be uppermost in our minds when we come to think or talk about him. It is this, in fact, which has become our starting point when we try to understand him. Our approach to Jesus today is very much that of the prologue of the gospel according to John:

In the beginning was the Word;
… and the Word was God.

... The Word was made flesh,
he lived among us,
and we saw his glory ... (1: 1ff).

In thinking about Jesus today, we start as it were 'from
above' and work 'downwards'.

Starting to understand Jesus 'from above' has, no doubt, its
advantages. For one thing it guarantees that we will never
forget the uniqueness of this human being. But it involves
some risk too. Once we start with the idea that Jesus was divine, our attention is immediately focused on this awesome
truth about him. The danger then is that we will be dazzled
by the divine. As a result we may fail to notice, or fail to take
seriously, the human in Jesus. But when this happens it becomes simply impossible for us to make any sense of Jesus
at all. Not only does it mean that we fail to take seriously the
human side of Jesus; it equally means that we can never
even begin to understand what the Christian community
means when it speaks of him as 'divine'. Since it is only in
and through the human that a divine reality can be seen to
shine forth in Jesus at all, it is only by taking Jesus seriously
as a real human being that we can have any hope of experiencing him as 'divine'.

An old story, a long history
The tendency to fail to take Jesus seriously as a human
being, or to regard the human side of him as of secondary
importance in the face of the divine, has a very long history
in the Church – something of which some Christians today
do not seem to be as conscious as they might be. Following
this long history can prove to be very rewarding.

The tendency referred to began to manifest itself almost
from the beginning of the Christian era – certainly from
once people had become accustomed to thinking or talking
of Jesus as 'divine'. It had appeared even by the end of the
century in which Jesus himself, this carpenter from Nazareth, lived and died. Even at that early stage there were

some who were so conscious of what they believed to be the divine presence in Jesus, and who also had such a poor view of the body and of matter generally, that they ceased to see Jesus as a real human being at all: God, these thought, could not really have taken to the divine Self anything as material as a human body; the human body of Jesus could have been no more than an appearance, a phantom! So, they put forward the view of Jesus known in the history books as *docetism*, but which today might be more intelligibly called 'phantomism' (a word used by Alan Richardson, author of *Creeds in the Making*). So it was that St Jerome was to write later:

> The blood of Christ was still fresh in Judea when his body was said to be a phantom (quoted by Alan Richardson in *Creeds In The Making*, p 36).

The tendency to fail to take Jesus seriously as a human being appeared again in the fourth century. Here a scholar and, indeed, a bishop, called Apollinarius, starting with the conviction that Jesus was divine, 'the Word of God made flesh', struggled to see how exactly the divine and human came together in Jesus. In his view Jesus was made up of a human body to which 'the Word of God' was united in such a way as to take the place of the human rational, spiritual faculty: Jesus was, we might say, 'a human body' in whom God did the thinking! In order to make place for the divine in Jesus, Apollinarius, then, sacrificed that which is specifically human in us all, our rational, spiritual faculty. In doing this, of course, he was really abandoning altogether the idea of Jesus being human.

In the following century the same tendency appeared once again. This time it found expression in a theory associated with Eutyches, a monk from Constantinople. For Eutyches too the starting point was that Jesus was divine. His aim was to explain how we could say that one and the same subject was both the man from Nazareth and 'the eternal Word

of God'. He explained it by saying that the human in Jesus
was somehow swallowed up by, and absorbed into, the
divine – 'dissolved like a drop of honey in the sea' as the
Concise Theological Dictionary puts it. He thus propounded
the 'single-nature' (*monophysite*) theory of Jesus. Of course,
in doing this Eutyches too sacrificed the human in Jesus so
as to make place for the divine: it takes only a little reflection to see that his view of Jesus comes very close to the earlier
'phantomism'.

Two centuries later, in the seventh century, a modified form
of the theory of Eutyches was suggested. This was associated
particularly with Sergius who was no less than the Patriarch
of Constantinople. For Sergius also the overriding truth
about Jesus was that he was God in our midst – he too approached Jesus 'from above'. In simple terms, his particular
concern was the very understandable one of showing that it
would have been impossible for this God-in-our-midst to
have sinned. To exclude this possibility, Sergius equivalently
removed from Jesus all human freedom: the human will of
Jesus, he maintained, was absorbed into the divine will –
Sergius thus propounded the 'single-will' (*monothelite*)
theory of Jesus. But in taking human freedom from Jesus he
too was saying that Jesus was not a real a human being at
all. Once again the human in Jesus was sacrificed in order to
leave room for the presence in him of the divine.

Jesus is 'truly human'
Just as we need to be aware today of the history of the tendency among Christians to fail to take Jesus seriously as a
human being, we need to be aware also, and *equally*, of the
nature, the consistency, and the firmness of the Christian
community's official reaction to it whenever it appeared.
Always this reaction was the same: always in its official
teaching the community emphatically affirmed that, even
though Jesus is believed to be 'the Word of God made flesh',
he was a *real, complete, human being* – in fact, as will become

clear, he was this precisely because he was the Word of God made flesh. This is a matter about which we cannot afford to have any doubts whatsoever: according to the Christian community's official teaching, Jesus is *fully* human. Fully human means not *ninety per cent* human, nor even *ninety-nine-point-nine-nine-nine per cent* human, but *one hundred per cent* human.

Thus 'phantomism' (*docetism*) was rejected frequently and firmly by recognised spokespeople like Ignatius of Antioch (c. 110) and, later, by the Council of Chalcedon (451). The views of Apollinarius and Eutyches were also firmly ruled out by the same Council. Sergius' teaching was rejected by the Sixth Council of Constantinople (680-81). The community's official position regarding Jesus being fully human is summarised in the perhaps archaic language of the Council of Chalcedon. According to this Council, Jesus, 'the eternal Word of God', is

> … complete in humanity … true man, … consisting of a rational soul and a body … of one substance with us in humanity, 'like us in all things apart from sin' (Heb 4: 15).

Jesus, the Church has long and consistently insisted, had, to use a very technical term to which we shall return at a later stage, a human 'nature'. By human 'nature', as the theology books were careful to explain, the Church means '*everything that makes a human being a human being*'.

An irony
There is, of course, a strange and, indeed, a sad irony here. That very point about Jesus which required no faith at all in those who knew him in the flesh, and which even his opponents would never have thought of denying, had to be declared a binding truth for people who later came to know him in faith as Son of God!

However, when we come to think about it, we can see that it is, perhaps, an understandable irony. The human is, after all, everyday and ordinary and commonplace, sometimes even boring. It can easily be taken for granted. The divine, on the other hand, seems to be beyond the ordinary and awesome. There is a temptation throughout all of life to belittle the ordinary, to by-pass the human, with its monotony, its struggle, its pain and its messiness, even at times to opt out of the earthly and to try to go 'directly' to God. In view of this we can hardly be all that surprised that once people came in faith to perceive the intensity of the presence of the divine in Jesus, they yielded, sometimes at least, to the temptation to regard the human in him as being of secondary importance, even to be almost irrelevant. The Christian community, however, has always in its most official teaching seen this tendency as false and futile: the only way in which we might possibly find God in Jesus, it has always insisted, is by taking seriously the human in all its everydayness and ordinariness. This, of course, is a point which is relevant not just to finding the divine in Jesus but to finding God in our own lives too.

Today: A double-think about Jesus?
Docetism and the views of people like Apollinarius, Eutyches and Sergius, no longer appear in the Church as formal theories regarding Jesus: there is nobody I know today who would set out to declare that Jesus of Nazareth only appeared to be human or that he was incomplete as a human being. Unfortunately, however, this does not mean that such ideas have totally disappeared from Church life. In fact, we find among Christians today a curious ambivalence about this human being, Jesus of Nazareth.

At the level of creed and formal profession of belief, there is 'a profound orthodoxy', to use Karl Rahner's phrase. At this level it seems never even to occur to Christians today to question the true humanness of Jesus: unhesitatingly they recite and subscribe to such creedal phrases as 'made flesh', 'true man', 'of one substance with us'. Their understanding of what these phrases are saying about Jesus is also, at an abstract level at least, without fault: they know that Jesus had, to use that technical term already referred to, a human 'nature' and that by this is meant *everything* which makes a human being a human being'.

It is when they come down to details about Jesus that the old tendency manifests itself again. We can notice it particularly, perhaps, in two attitudes which are very common – attitudes which need to be referred to at this point even though they will be examined in greater detail in later chapters.

The first is the ease with which some people seem to be able to attribute to Jesus characteristics which, on reflection, can be seen to be incompatible with being human. For example, some seem to find it easy to think of Jesus as having had unlimited power at his finger-tips and, so, to be able to do anything he might have wanted to do. To illustrate this, I might cite a remark made during an adult religious education session recently. At the end of the session, after we had spent an hour reflecting on a gospel-passage in which Jesus was interacting with an infirm woman and with a religious opponent (Lk 13:10ff), a lady in the group said, by way of bringing our discussion to a simple conclusion: 'But anyway Jesus was infinite'! The sense in which this statement can have an orthodox meaning will become clear in the course of the following chapters. What ought to be clear even now is that there is one sense in which it certainly cannot be orthodox. If it is implying that the human being, Jesus of Nazareth was not *really* immersed in our struggle to be compassionate and outspoken, then it is equivalently saying that he was not really one of us at all. In that case it is, of course, implying that in him the 'eternal Word' did not really become 'incarnate'. When attributes like omnipotence are attributed in this simple way to Jesus, it is clear that, when all is said, he is not being thought of as a human being but is actually being removed from the realm of the human.

The second example is the rather common tendency to see

the human reality in Jesus as being so overshadowed by the divine as to be altogether devoid of its own human spontaneity, freedom, independence and personality. It is the tendency to see the human reality in Jesus as, to quote the German theologian, Walter Kasper:

> ... basically only a kind of clothing behind which God himself speaks and acts (*Jesus The Christ*, p 46).

If we can think of the human in Jesus in this way, then obviously – despite what we profess in the creed – we are not thinking of him as a human being at all; rather we understand him as a human 'puppet on strings', to use Karl Rahner's phrase. Indeed I myself find it interesting that Apollinarius' understanding of Jesus strikes strong chords in the minds of many Catholics today. Quite often, after I have explained the mistaken way in which Apollinarius understood the coming together of the divine and human in Jesus, people have said to me that they too have always thought of Jesus as a human being in whom God did the thinking and talking – in other words, that they have understood him in apollinarian terms. Of course, thinking of Jesus in this way is not altogether without its attractions. To believe that in Jesus God actually takes our human nature, even in its bodiliness, to the divine Self, is not at all always easy for us to accept. It may well involve a change not just in our thinking about Jesus, but also in our attitudes towards ourselves – a point which the American theologian, Brian O. McDermott makes:

> The conversion that is required to change this perception is not always, exclusively, an intellectual change of mind, the graduation to a better theology; it may rather be a healing of the heart concerning the value of one's own humanity in the face of God and before the tribunal of one's own self (*Word Become Flesh*, p 202).

The fact, however, is that when, for whatever reason, we today fail to take Jesus seriously as a human being, we are doing in our own way what the 'phantomists' and Apollinarius and Eutyches and Sergius did in their way in their day. What we are setting out to do is, of course, most praiseworthy: our intention is to be faithful to, and to uphold, the awesome truth about Jesus being 'divine' – *at least as we understand this doctrine*. We want to defend the 'divinity of Jesus' at all costs. The fact is, of course, that we may not defend this at all costs. If, for example, we find ourselves defending it at the cost of the human in Jesus, then we are not defending it at all. For if our understanding of the 'divinity' is such that it forces us to take away even a fraction of a percentage from what would make Jesus a real human being, then, as ought to be clear from history, we have not really understood this truth about him at all – at least not as the Christian community in its official teaching understands and has always understood it. We are, in fact, in that case upholding and defending something which we really should not be upholding or defending but which we should, rather, be opposing. While setting out with the loyal and pious desire to be orthodox, we end up, ironically, defending what amounts to heresy! Indeed it is the opinion of Karl Rahner that many people today who reject what they hear Christians saying about Christ, reject, not the true Christian position at all, but rather a misrepresentation and, consequently, a false version of it: they reject a version which even Christians themselves, if they knew the truth, ought to reject. What Rahner says in this context is worth quoting:

> The idea exists that God disguises himself as a man, or that needing to make himself visible, he makes gestures by means of a human reality which is used in such a way that it is not *a real man with independence and freedom*, but a puppet on strings which the player behind the scenes uses to make himself audible. But this is mythology, and not Church dogma, even though it may be a fair description of the catechism in many Christians' heads in con-

trast to the printed catechism. ... And it may be that some non-Christians are thus led to rely on a cryptogamous heresy of Christians..., thinking ... that it is a dogma of Christianity. (*Theological Investigations*, vol 4, p 118, italics mine).

There is another way

The reason why Christians fail so often today to think of Jesus as a real human being has, I believe, a lot to do with their starting point. The truth about him of which they are most conscious is not so much that he is a human being, but that he is 'a divine person'. They think of him first and foremost as '*God* become man'. Their starting point is 'from above'.

This, of course, is not the only possible starting point. The first disciples approached Jesus, we ought to remember, without any presuppositions whatsoever about his being 'divine'. They first got to know and to admire a human being, Jesus, a man from Nazareth. They followed him around, listened to him, observed him interacting with people, saw him praying, watched him being put to death, suffer and die, and, above all, experienced him as being brought through death to a new life. It was as a result of this contact with him that they came – slowly and very gradually, as we shall see – to believe that, to use words attributed to the centurion in the gospel according to Mark,

In truth this man was son of God (15: 39).

While we today start 'from above' and work (or try to work) 'downwards', they started 'from below' and worked 'upwards'. Because they started 'from below', they, unlike us, could never lose sight of the fact that Jesus was and remained a human being.

The task today

Obviously it is not possible for us today, almost two thousand years later, to follow exactly the faith-journey of these first disciples. We do not, and cannot, meet Jesus in the flesh. I am convinced, however, that unless we too begin to think about Jesus as they did, we have no hope of understanding him at all – either as 'son of man' *or* as 'Son of God'. Consequently we will not be able to explain – or to hand on – true faith about him to others.

Trying to help people to know *what kind* of human being Jesus was is something on which a lot of time and energy is spent in Christian preaching and teaching today: we emphasise, for example, how compassionate and kind and loving and committed Jesus was, particularly with regard to the poor. This, of course, is as it should be: in the Christian view, Jesus is, after all, the perfect model of human living. It seems to me, however, that, today at least, the more fundamental and urgent task which needs to be done is that of helping people to think of Jesus first of all as *really* being a member of our race. It is, after all, rather difficult to appreciate the quality of a human life, and to take this life seriously as a model of living, if we are not convinced that what is in question is a human life at all! It is difficult to do this if, for example, when we are reflecting on the compassion of Jesus or on his struggle with the religious leaders of his day, we all the time have at the back of our minds the notion that he, after all, was infinite and, being infinite, was not really one of us.

It is with this more basic and urgent task that this book is concerned.

The two-button trap
It is my experience that very often the person who sets out with the intention of taking Jesus seriously as a human being needs, today especially, to be warned of what I call 'the two-button trap' along the way.

In order to bring home to people that Jesus was not an all-powerful god 'masquerading' behind a human form, but was really a humble human being, the limitations which

Jesus experienced have to be emphasised. The reader might quite readily go along with all that is being said about these: *'As a human being'*, he or she might think, 'Jesus must, of course, have experienced all these limitations. But *as God* he could not have experienced weakness.' What the reader might mean by this is all-important. He or she might mean that the man Jesus somehow had two systems available to him, a human one and a divine one, being able, as it were, to press button A, which would give him access to human powers and to a human mode of acting, or button B, which would give him access to divine powers and to a divine mode of acting. The reader would in that case think that what is being said about Jesus now is being said about him 'as man', but might be waiting for him to be discussed at a later stage 'as God' when the focus would be on an unlimited side of him. He or she might expect – and here would be walking into the trap – that something would be said about Jesus then which would somehow compensate for, or even equivalently eliminate, his limitations.

The person who thinks like this has not, of course, really begun to approach Jesus as a human being. In giving him access to two 'systems', in making two 'buttons' available to him to operate and control, the person has once again taken Jesus out of the realm of the human. The simple fact is that human beings do not have two systems available to them or two buttons to press. Even if it were possible to imagine 'someone' having two such systems, two modes of operating, it would be simply impossible to think of this 'someone' as a human being. Were Jesus to have two 'systems' available to him in the way described, he would be more than human. But he would be more than human *in such a way as not to be really human at all*! What Macbeth said, albeit in a very different context, would be true of him:

> I dare do all that may become a man;
> Who dares do more is none (Act 1: Scene 7).

This is not to say that Jesus, through the power of God,

could not have performed signs and wonders – as, indeed, the scriptures describe other human beings, like Peter and Paul, doing (e.g. Acts, 3:1f; 14:8f; 20:7f). But it is to say that if we do not see Jesus as a real human being, then the Jesus we are imagining is neither the Jesus of history nor the Christ of the faith of the Church. When, therefore, it can be truthfully said that Jesus of Nazareth, being a humble human being, experienced all the limitations which necessarily go with this, then nothing can be said about God's eternal 'Son made flesh' which would take from this truth or make it irrelevant.

* * *

The first small step onto the moon was described at the time as also a giant leap. It is my experience that the same might be said about the first step which needs to be taken by many even devout Christians today if they are to begin to understand the one who is at the very centre of their faith, Jesus of Nazareth. To think of the man from Nazareth first as a member of our race, and really to see him as such, would indeed seem to be a small step for anyone to have to take. I find, however, that for many Christians today it is, in fact, a giant leap. Those who do take it find that they can then discover, in a new and exciting way, the truth about this man Jesus and what it means to say that he is *Emmanuel*, that is, God-with-us.

The Gospels

CHAPTER TWO

A Church without gospels

The gospels are the most sacred, the most inspiring and the most important documents about Jesus. Every piece of writing, however, if it is to be understood properly and used properly, needs to be taken seriously as the kind of writing which it is. A poem, for example, needs to be read and used as a poem. To read or to quote it as a straightforward piece of history would be to misread and to misuse it: we could then find ourselves believing – and perhaps trying to lead others to believe – that, for example, G.K. Chesterton has propounded the following historical thesis: that fishes once flew, that forests once walked, that figs once grew on thorns, that there once was a moment which the moon was not what we now know it to be, but blood, and that it was at that moment that the animal we know as the donkey was born!

What is true of literature generally is equally true of the gospels. If we are to understand these properly, and if we are to use them properly, we need to understand the kind of writing with which we are dealing. Otherwise we will inevitably find ourselves taking them as saying – and most probably quoting them as saying – what they never really intended to say at all. When this happens, then those very documents which are meant to help us to understand Jesus will, sadly, become a hindrance to our doing so.

An adequate understanding of the gospels, important as they are in Christian faith, cannot at all be presumed among Christians today. Indeed it is my experience that, generally speaking, Catholics at least, have a very inadequate understanding of these crucial documents. For the most part they still seem to think of them – and to quote them – as four straightforward factual accounts of the words and deeds of Jesus – as four straightforward biographies of Jesus. Very often they seem to think of them as one such account. So, in religious discussions I often come up against an argument which begins 'But doesn't the gospel say ...', and which goes on to quote 'the gospel' as if 'it' were a straightforward report of something which Jesus said or did exactly as described. The facts are, however, that there are four gospels, not just one, and that these are not by any means straightforward accounts of the life of Jesus. They are very complex documents and very different from any other writings with which most of us are likely to be familiar. The person who misses this point will find it very difficult, indeed impossible, to come to a correct theological understanding of Jesus: he or she will find it very difficult to think of Jesus as being genuinely, really and fully human and, so, will never understand him.

If, then, we are to begin to understand Jesus 'from below' we need at the outset to be sure that we are aware of the unique nature of these important but very unusual documents.

To understand the gospels, we need to know how, in general terms at least, they came to be. As modern biblical scholarship has shown, the story of the gospels' coming-to-be is a very long and complicated one. This is a point which the 1964 *Instruction* of the Vatican's Pontifical Biblical Commission, *The Historical Truth of the Gospels*, has acknowledged – though strangely, and regrettably, the contents of this important document do not seem to have been communicated at all in everyday Catholic teaching, not to mention in ordinary preaching. This chapter sets out to tell, as briefly and as faithfully as possible, this long but interesting and very important story.

A long process of coming-to-be

Most scholars today are of the view that the first of our four gospels to be written was Mark (not, as the order of our Bible might suggest, Matthew). It was written around the years 68-70 c.e. The final edition of the last, the gospel according to John, was made around 100 c.e. Between the birth of Jesus and the completion of our gospels there was, then, approximately a whole century. The 1964 Pontifical *Instruction*, following the findings of scholars of the Bible, acknowledges three distinct stages in this century-long process of the coming-to-be of the gospels. Since it so happens that each of the three stages took somewhat over thirty years, we can divide the first century of the Christian era into thirds and think, with Raymond E. Brown, the distinguished American Roman Catholic biblical scholar, of each stage as corresponding to one of the thirds.

The first stage

Before the gospels, and eventually giving rise to them, there was, of course, the life, ministry, death and resurrection of Jesus of Nazareth. Since without this there would not be gospels at all, this, as the *Instruction* points out, is the first stage in the process of gospel-formation, the first 'layer' in the gospel tradition. Jesus' life corresponds roughly to the first third of the first century.

The second stage

Had the gospels been written immediately after the death and resurrection of Jesus they might have been straightforward documents. But in that case they would have been very different documents from those which God actually willed the Church to have and which the Christian community now cherishes as 'the gospels'. Presuming that the gospel according to Mark was not written until around 68-70 c.e., roughly a third of a century elapsed between the death of Jesus and the first gospel. This pre-gospel period was, briefly, one in which the early disciples proclaimed Jesus and, in the process, also came to understand him more fully. It was one in which there emerged an understanding of Jesus, and a way of proclaiming him, which constituted what can be called a 'Jesus tradition'. This 'Jesus tradition' had as its origin and source the preaching and proclamation of the original apostles who were eyewitnesses to the events proclaimed, and it was now available to those who joined, or succeeded, them as preachers of the Good News.

The third stage

The final stage in the formation of the gospels was the actual compilation of the gospels themselves. What happened here was that between roughly 70 and 100 c.e., four people ('evangelists'), living in different places, took the 'Jesus tradition' which had emerged in the second stage, and compiled it into the four documents which we know as the four 'gospels'. This took place during the last third of the first century.

The story of the coming-to-be of the gospels, beginning, as it did, with the life of Jesus, and ending with the compilation of John around the year 100, was, then, a century-long one.

The 'Jesus Tradition'

The 'Jesus tradition' which emerged in the second stage was the quarry out of which the material for the gospels was hewn. If we are to deepen our understanding of what kind of documents the gospels are, obviously we need to know something about this 'tradition' and how it emerged in this period.

1. Jesus was *understood*

We who have inherited a long tradition of belief about Jesus can find it difficult to visualise the situation of the first disciples. We might, of course, unthinkingly assume that they too were handed a ready-made understanding of him. We would, however, be naïve in assuming this. In fact, these early disciples only gradually came to understand Jesus. To have some sense of how they grew in understanding, we need to focus immediately on the *resurrection*.

The role of the resurrection

Here again it is not always easy for one who is familiar with the centuries-long belief in Jesus's resurrection to appreciate what an astonishing experience the resurrection was for the first disciples. Jesus was dead – and buried. Yet the disciples experienced him to be still present to them and with them! They did not, of course, experience him to be with them now in the same way as he had been with them before – they did not think of the resurrection in the way that Lazarus' coming back to life might be thought of (nor should we think of it in this way). Their experience was that Jesus, though dead, had been brought through death by God to a new 'life', that God had, as it was imaginatively put, 'seated him at his own right hand', and that Jesus was now present with them in a real and powerful, though new, way. So unexpected and astonishing was this experience that the disciples found it very difficult to come to terms with it. The story of the disciples on the road to Emmaus gives us a sense of their reaction: it brings out their disappointment, disillusionment, even despondency at his death, their astonishment and puzzlement at the rumours that he was 'alive', and their joy and surprise at their own altogether unexpected encounter with him (Lk 24: 13ff).

The effect which the resurrection had on how the disciples understood Jesus could easily escape us. We can best appreciate it, I think, if we consider first, and in some detail, the role it played in their understanding of Jesus' identity.

Who is this man?

If we are used to taking the gospels at their face value we might think that the disciples were fully aware of Jesus' identity – his identity, as they believed, as 'Son of God' – all through the period of his ministry. We might recall, for example, the accounts of his conception, birth, baptism and

transfiguration and some of the discourses attributed to
him in John, where this 'divine Sonship' is clearly acknowledged. We might recall, for instance, Matthew's account of
the transfiguration:

> ... a bright cloud covered them with shadow, and from
> the cloud there came a voice which said, 'This my Son,
> the Beloved; he enjoys my favour. Listen to him (17: 5).

Or we might recall that in John we find Jesus himself saying
early in his ministry:

> Yes, God loved the world so much
> that he gave his only Son,
> so that everyone who believes in him may not be lost
> but may have eternal life.
> For God sent his Son into the world
> not to condemn the world,
> but so that through him the world might be saved
> (Jn 3: 16-17).

We might think that the fact that the 'divine Sonship' is acknowledged in gospel-passages like these means that this
had been clearly revealed to the disciples during the life of
Jesus. The evidence, however, is that this was not at all the
case.

Through careful study of the Christian scriptures as a whole
(and not just of the gospels), scholars are able to get behind
the pages of the gospels and to catch glimpses of what went
on in that third of a century after the death of Jesus before
our gospels were compiled. They are able, for example, to
point to four particularly important stages in the development of the disciples' understanding of Jesus' identity. If we
look even briefly at these four stages, we will get an insight
into the process of development which was going on in this
crucial period of the Church's history.

Sonship and resurrection
In regard to understanding who Jesus really was, the evidence is that it was the *resurrection* that was the real moment

of truth for the disciples. Before the resurrection they had, of course, believed that God was at work and present in Jesus – it was on account of this that they had become his followers. But it was their experience of him as 'the risen Lord' that brought them to a full realisation of who he was – it was the *resurrection* that brought them to understand what is now called the 'divine Sonship' of Jesus.

The point which is of most interest to us here is that in their early preaching it was with the *resurrection* that the disciples associated this Sonship of Jesus. Scholars find hints and echoes of this primitive apostolic proclamation in passages like the following from sermons in the Acts of the Apostles and from the letters written to the early Christian communities. A close reading of these texts shows that this first proclamation spoke of Jesus as one who through the resurrection was 'made' and 'exalted as' 'Lord' and 'Christ' and 'Saviour', and was 'begotten' and 'designated' as 'Son'.

Peter, for example, is presented in the following passage in the Acts of the Apostles as linking with the resurrection Jesus' *reception of the Holy Spirit* and his being made *Lord*, and *Christ*:

> God raised this man Jesus to life ... Now raised to the heights by God's right hand, he has received from the Father the Holy Spirit, who was promised ... God has made this Jesus whom you crucified both Lord and Christ (Acts 2: 32-36).

In another passage Peter is represented as linking with the resurrection Jesus' title as *Saviour*:

> By his own right hand God has now raised him up to be leader and saviour ... (Acts 5: 31).

Another passage in Acts represents Paul as associating Jesus' divine *Sonship* with the resurrection:

> It was to our ancestors that God made the promise but it is to us, their children, that he has fulfilled it, by raising

Jesus from the dead. As scripture says in the first psalm: *You are my son; today I have become your father* (Acts 13: 32-33).

In his Letter to the Romans Paul himself speaks of Jesus as being proclaimed *Son of God* in the resurrection:

> This news is about the Son of God who, according to the human nature he took, was a descendant of David: it is about Jesus Christ our Lord who, in the order of the spirit, the spirit of holiness that was in him, was proclaimed Son of God in all his power through his resurrection from the dead (Rom 1:3-4).

Indeed in this passage some scholars believe Paul to be using what was actually an early form of the Christian creed.

In the Letter to the Philippians the *Lordship* of Jesus is associated with the resurrection:

> ... he was humbler yet,
> even to accepting death,
> death on a cross.
> But God raised him high
> and gave him the name
> which is above all other names
> ... Lord (Phil 2: 8-11).

Originally, then, the great insight into who Jesus was – what scholars tend to call 'the christological moment' – came with the *resurrection*, and it was with the *resurrection* that the the disciples, early in their preaching, linked his becoming Son.

Sonship and Jesus' baptism

Reflection, however, showed the disciples the limitation of this understanding of Jesus. What Jesus was now, had he not been before? If he was Son of God in the resurrection, had he not been Son all during their years with him – all during his public life? The realization that he had been, led to a further stage of development in understanding Jesus' identity. What followed was, to use a phrase of the Irish scholar, Wilfrid Harrington, 'a casting back' to Jesus during his ministry, of the understanding, and even of the titles, first associated with the *risen* Christ.

The moment of Jesus's revelation by the Father as his beloved Son was, in this stage, pushed from the resurrection back to the beginning of Jesus' ministry when he was baptised by John. We have an echo of this stage in understanding in Mark. This, very probably the earliest gospel, begins with the Baptist's preaching followed immediately by Jesus' baptism in the Jordan (Mark, like John, does not have any account at all of the infancy of Jesus). Mark makes it clear to the reader from the outset that even at his baptism in the Jordan, Jesus was Son:

> No sooner had he come out of the water than he saw the heavens torn apart and the Spirit, like a dove, descending on him. And a voice came from heaven, 'You are my Son, the Beloved; my favour rests on you (Mk. 1: 10-11).

So, while the first preaching linked Jesus' reception of the Holy Spirit and his being proclaimed 'Son of God' (Acts 2: 32-3 and Rom 1: 4) with the resurrection, Mark emphasises that already at his baptism by John these events had occurred for Jesus. (Some scholars recognise in Mark's account of the baptism an echo of that early creed used by Paul in his Letter to the Romans and referred to above.) In this second stage of understanding, echoed in this passage in Mark, 'the christological moment' has been pushed back from the resurrection to the beginning of Jesus' ministry.

Sonship and Jesus' conception

As we would expect, reflection on Jesus continued. As it did, the limitations of this stage in understanding were also shown up. Why think of Jesus as becoming Son of God only at the beginning of his public ministry? If he was Son, surely he was Son from the beginning of his existence as a human being? It was at this point of reflection and development,

the evidence is, that interest in the infancy of Jesus arose
and that infancy stories began to be told – a stage of development which is reflected in the gospels of Matthew and
Luke, the only gospels with infancy accounts. A point
which we find is strongly emphasised throughout both
these stories is that Jesus was the Son of God *from the first
moment of his conception*. So, while the first proclamation
associated the coming of the Spirit on Jesus with the resurrection, it is now made clear that Jesus was *conceived* by the
Holy Spirit. While titles like 'Christ', 'Saviour' and 'Lord'
were originally linked with the resurrection, now, the shep-
herds are told in Luke, Jesus has these titles from his birth:

> Today ... a saviour has been born to you; he is Christ the
> Lord (Lk 2: 11; cf Mt 1: 21).

In the stage of the disciples' understanding reflected here,
Jesus did not have to wait for his resurrection, or even for
his baptism, to be 'begotten' as Son, but was so from his *conception*: Mary is told in Luke:

> You are to conceive and bear a son ... He will be great
> and will be called Son of the Most High (Lk 1: 32).

The 'christological moment' is now pushed back to the conception. As Joseph A. Fitzmyer puts it:

> What was kerygmatically proclaimed about Jesus' rela-
> tion to David and to the Spirit *as of the resurrection* was in
> time pressed back to his very conception in the tradition
> that both Matthew and Luke inherited from the Christian
> community (*A Christological Catechism*, p 33).

Pre-existent Son
Further reflection – reflection on the eternal existence of
God's 'Son' – led to another important insight. If Jesus was
really God's Son, then surely there is an eternal aspect to
Jesus. So, in a further stage of development in understand-
ing, Jesus' identity is seen as reaching back to that of the
'Word' 'before' creation: Jesus is seen as the 'pre-existent'

Son of God. 'The christological moment' is pushed back
from the conception to *eternal existence* with God. This is a
stage of development which is clearly reflected in John, the
last of our gospels. The prologue of this gospel, as is well
known, begins before the infancy:

> In the beginning was the Word;
> the Word was with God
> and the Word was God.
> ...
> The Word was made flesh,
> he lived among us ... (Jn 1: 1ff).

John, passing over the infancy in silence, then goes on to the
public life. In presenting this life, he portrays Jesus as speaking openly 'as a pre-existent divine figure' (8: 58; 10: 30; 14:
9; 17: 5): this is a most important characteristic of John's gospel and one to which I shall return.

What took place in those early years was, then, in Raymond
E. Brown's phrase, 'a backwards-growth' in christology.

A fuller understanding of the words and deeds of Jesus
The resurrection, it is important to know, especially in our
present context, influenced much more than the disciples'
understanding of Jesus' identity. It influenced also their understanding of what he had *said and done* before the resurrection and what had really been happening during their
years with him. Now they could look back on what had
gone before and reflect on it in a new light – in the light of
who they *now* understood Jesus to be and of the definitive
place which they now believed he had in God's plan. As
they reflected on it in this new light, they began to see the
full significance of what had been happening. They now
found that words and deeds and events had a meaning that
they had not appreciated, or at least had not fully appreciated, before. They came, in the words of the Pontifical *Instruction*, to 'a fuller understanding' of these (no. 2).

The 'backwards' movement characterised the whole process of their understanding of Jesus; the influence of the resurrection on their understanding of Jesus was profound and all-pervasive.

2. Jesus is *Proclaimed*

We come closer to understanding our gospels when we realise that the influence of the resurrection extended also to the way in which Jesus was *proclaimed* during this pre-gospel period. With regard to this there are four points in particular of which we need to be aware.

From a resurrection perspective

The first, and by far the most important point, concerns the *perspective* from which the story of Jesus was proclaimed. To understand this we need to remember why it was that the disciples proclaimed Jesus at all. They proclaimed him because of – and only because of – the significance which they now knew him to have in God's plan. In proclaiming him, therefore, what they wanted to do was to share with others their experience of him, and their faith in him, as *the risen one*, and, so, as the one they *now* knew to be *the Messiah* ('the Christ'), 'the Son of God', 'Saviour', 'Lord' (to use their own language). In no way were they interested in simply telling the story of Jesus 'just as it happened' or even just as they experienced and understood it while it was happening. What they were interested in doing was to proclaim to all the full meaning of the story as they now understood it, the story as they understood it in hind-sight, in resurrection-sight, in faith-sight. During these years Jesus was, then, proclaimed with a faith-purpose and *from a resurrection per--spective.*

This is not to say, as the Vatican Instruction warns against saying, that in this post-resurrection proclamation, Jesus

> ... was transformed into a 'mythical' personage, and his teaching distorted by reason of the worship which the disciples now paid him, revering him as Lord and Son of God (no. 2).

But it is to say, as Raymond E. Brown puts it, that

> ... there was no attempt to report with simple, uncolored factuality what Jesus had said and done. Rather the report was *enlightened by a faith that the preachers wanted to share* (*Responses to 101 Questions on the Bible* , p 56; italics mine).

It is to say, as Joseph A. Fitzmyer says, that

> ... none of these disciple-preachers ever sought to reproduce with factual accuracy the words and deeds of Jesus himself; they understood those words and deeds with hindsight and adapted them to the needs of those to whom they preached (*A Christological Catechism*, p 25).

It is to say, as the *Instruction* says, that 'in the light of that fuller understanding which they enjoyed', the Apostles

> ... in their turn interpreted his words and deeds according to the needs of their hearers (no. 2).

A complex form of proclamation
The second point which needs to be noted is the *form* which the tradition about Jesus took in this period.

Obviously the Good News about him was handed on first of all in the form of *preaching*. But this preaching, as we can well imagine, could never have consisted simply in straight prose. In experiencing Jesus as risen and as Lord, the disciples had been brought, as the biblical scholar C.H. Dodd says,

> ... to the frontiers of normal human experience, where experience runs out into mystery (*The Founder of Christianity*, p 29).

To communicate such an experience they had to stretch language and to resort to whatever imagery and symbol was available to them. This, as we know, was available to them in plenty in the rich heritage of their Jewish scriptures.

The Good News was transmitted through *catechesis* too. For

catechetical purposes the early preachers resorted to memory aids, so necessary in an age where writing material was scarce. They therefore used such techniques as grouping together sayings and parables of Jesus and stories of his deeds in a way that these could easily be remembered and taught.

A further point which we need to remember is, of course, that Jesus was not just talked about during these years. He was also *worshipped* and *celebrated*. The eucharist, for example, was being celebrated long before the gospels were written – the earliest account of the eucharist in scripture is found in Paul's First Letter to the Corinthians which predates the gospels. It was through this worship too in its various forms – liturgy, prayers, hymns, and so on – as well as through preaching and catechesis in its various forms, that the Good News about Jesus was communicated and experienced during these pre-gospel years.

The form, then, in which the early disciples communicated their resurrection-faith in Jesus was very complex and rich indeed. The need to be aware of the complexity of the form which this pre-gospel tradition took, and the importance of taking it into account for understanding the gospels, is a point which is strongly emphasised by the 1964 *Instruction*:

> These varied ways of speaking which the heralds of Christ made use of in proclaiming him, must be distinguished one from the other and carefully appraised: catecheses, narratives, testimonies, hymns, doxologies, prayers and any other such forms as were customarily employed in Sacred Scripture and by people at the time (no. 2).

This emphasis of the *Instruction* is, of course, very understandable: obviously the way in which we are to understand, for example, what a hymn about Jesus is saying is very different from the way in which we are to understand a precise theological statement about him.

A translated message

A third point which needs to be adverted to is the process of *translation* which was going on in these years. The period in question was one of rapid expansion for the young Church. The Good News about Jesus was being preached now not just in the Jewish world of Jerusalem and Galilee, but in the Greek-influenced world of cities like Corinth and Ephesus, and in Rome itself, the very heart of the Roman world. So, in order to make the message intelligible and alive for new audiences, a lot of translation had to take place. This, of course, included, as well as translation into different languages, adaptation to new cultures.

'Second generation' preachers

A fourth and final point, and one which is of great relevance for our understanding of the gospels, is that now Jesus was no longer being preached by the original disciples and witnesses only. At this stage these were being joined by people who had not themselves heard or seen Jesus but who were relying for the Good News on what they had received from the original eyewitnesses. These were people to whom Raymond E. Brown refers as 'second generation Christians'.

* * *

The four gospels are a very important and familiar feature of Church life today. So much so, that we might assume that they were always there and we might find it difficult to imagine a Church which existed without them. We might even think that these were the documents on which the Church was based. The fact is, however, that for a third of a century after the resurrection, there was a Church but not yet any of our four gospels. Some writings concerning Jesus may indeed have existed in this period – for example, there is evidence that Matthew and Luke draw, not just on Mark, but also on another important source which has not survived. The period was, however, one in which the Good News of Jesus was communicated for the most part orally.

What concerns us here is to ensure that a misunderstanding of the gospels will not be the cause of our failure to take Jesus seriously as a human being. What needs to be kept in mind most of all is, therefore, that the 'Jesus tradition' which was developed during the pre-gospel years did not concentrate on giving a straight-forward *Life of Jesus* but presented, rather, in preaching and in worship, the *Gospel* of Jesus, or, as the underlying Greek word suggests, the *Good News* about him.

CHAPTER THREE

When a help
can become a hindrance

To think that the gospels bring us back, *in a direct way*, to Jesus himself as he lived in history would be very wrong. In trying to interpret the gospels, the most serious mistake we could make would be to underestimate the importance in the process of their formation of the 'Jesus tradition' which was developed during the first thirty or so years of the Church's life. Far from ignoring or by-passing it, the four gospels are in fact four compilations of this very tradition:

> The sacred authors, for the benefit of the churches, took this earliest body of instruction ... and set it down in the four gospels (The 1964 Vatican *Instruction*, no. 2).

The intimate link which there is between the gospels and the 'Jesus tradition' described in the previous chapter, is expressed by Raymond E. Brown in the following lines from his description of a gospel:

> ... I would describe a gospel as containing a distillation from the tradition about Jesus, involving his words, deeds, passion, death, and resurrection. This distillation was organized ... by an evangelist in the last third of the first century ... (*Responses to 101 Questions on the Bible*, pp 57-8).

The importance of this tradition in the coming-to-be of the gospels becomes very obvious when we consider that it may well have been the only source to which any of the four compilers of the gospels had access. Today it is clear that we have to reckon with the possibility at least (scholars say the high probability) that *none* of the four evangelists were themselves eyewitnesses to the words and deeds of Jesus

but were 'second generation Christians' – contrary though
this is to many current traditions and popular beliefs about
the four evangelists. As 'second generation Christians', the
evangelists would therefore have been relying for their gos-
pel-material totally on the tradition of which I have been
speaking.

To see, then, or to quote, a gospel as being a straightforward
Life of Jesus which always simply recounts words as they
were actually said, and deeds always as they were exactly
done, and events always exactly as they happened, would
be to make a most serious mistake. Joseph A. Fitzmyer expresses the seriousness of such a mistake in very strong
terms, going so far as to say that it would be 'suicide':

> To pretend that Stage III (*i.e. what is recounted in the gos-
> pels*) equals Stage I (*i.e. the actual life of Jesus*) is a form of
> naïvete. It can have disastrous effects eventually, as has
> often been attested: either intellectual suicide (a refusal to
> think and use one's intellect, God's greatest natural gift to
> human beings) or a total loss of faith (a failure to follow
> where his Spirit guides the Christian community) (*A
> Christological Catechism*, p 28, italicised words mine).

Yet it is a mistake which many Christians are still making,
or, perhaps, a form of intellectual and faith suicide which
they are committing. Furthermore, despite the 1964 Vatican
Instruction, it is something which they do not seem to be
helped to avoid. The result of this, as far as our present topic
is concerned, is that they find it very difficult, if not impossible, to take Jesus seriously as a human being.

An example will make this very clear. In John we read of the
man Jesus speaking as one who is conscious of existing before he was born of Mary, one who had, in that pre-existent
state, experienced the 'heavenly' life of God, and who has
now come down on earth. So, we read of Jesus praying:

> Now, Father, it is time for you to glorify me

with that glory I had with you
before ever the world was (Jn 17: 5).

We read also of him saying to 'the Jews',

I tell you most solemnly,
before Abraham ever was,
I Am (Jn 8: 58).

Obviously if we take this gospel as straight biography, and
understand passages like these as implying that Jesus of
Nazareth was conscious of living with God before he was
born of Mary, then we are going to find it difficult – to put it
very mildly indeed – to think of Jesus as anything other than
God not in our midst, but in a mask, a human mask. And if
we are thinking of Jesus in this way, then we are thinking of
him in some kind of *docetist* or *phantomist* way – a way of understanding him which, as we know, had to be, and was in
fact, rejected by the Christian community very early in its
history. If we do find ourselves in this position, it is important that we know why: the reason is that we are forgetting,
or that we do not know, that John, no more that the tradition of which it is a compilation, does not at all set out to
give a straight *Life of Jesus* in the sense of a modern biography. Like the other gospels, it sets out, rather, to present,
with the needs of a particular audience in mind, what the
tradition on which it is drawing had set out to do: it sets out
to proclaim the Good News – the gospel – of Jesus Christ.
Forgetting this, or not knowing it, we fail to take into account the all-important fact that John, like the other gospels,
is not at all primarily biographical, but rather theological.
And, of course, once we fail to take this into account, we inevitably, at some stage or other, misunderstand this writer.
Not taking into account his purpose in writing, or the
nature of his presentation, we take his words literally and at
face value. We then take him to be saying about Jesus as he
lived in history what, with a deeper understanding of the
text, we would know he is not at all actually saying. When

this happens we are, of course, in a position similar to that of a person who, reading Chesterton in a very superficial way, takes him as saying that it really was at a time when fishes were flying and forests were walking that the donkey was born!

Four different gospels

I have taken the gospel according to John as an example here on purpose. To appreciate why, we need to reflect, briefly, on another aspect of the gospels, that is, the individuality of each one.

Even though all four gospels are compilations of the body of tradition about Jesus which had emerged during that crucial second third of the first century, each compilation has its own unique character. Each was made by a different person, at a different time, in a different place, and with the needs of a particular audience in mind. So, Raymond E. Brown, after describing a gospel as 'a distillation of the tradition about Jesus, involving his words, deeds, passion, death and resurrection', as quoted above, adds:

> This distillation was organized, edited, and reshaped by an evangelist in the last third of the first century in order to address the spiritual needs of Christian readers he envisaged (as above, p 58).

In order to meet the real needs of his audience, each evangelist put his own stamp on the material available to him. As the 1964 *Instruction* says,

> They *selected* certain things out of the many which had been handed on; some they *synthesized*, some they *explained* with an eye to the situation of the churches, painstakingly using every means of bringing home to their readers the solid truth of the things in which they had been instructed. ... the sacred authors selected especially those items which were adapted to the varied circumstances of the faithful as well as to the end which they themselves wished to attain ... (no. 2, italics mine).

So, even though the four gospels have, naturally, much in common – for one thing, each was a compilation of a tradition which was based ultimately on the witnesses of the apostles – still all four give their own version of the Good News. The result is that we have in the four gospels, four different presentations of the Good News, and four different portraits of the same Christ of Christian faith. So – as I have already said at the beginning of the previous chapter – it is important to remember that we have four different gospels, not just one.

The gospel according to John – a note

The way Jesus is presented in John is particularly distinctive and needs to be commented on here for two reasons.

The Jesus of John

The first has to do with the particular presentation of the Christ of Christian faith which we have in that gospel. John, it will be recalled, was the last gospel to be compiled. It was written in, and for, a community (probably in Ephesus) which had evolved a 'high', or highly developed, christology and it represents very clearly the latest stage in the early Church's understanding of Jesus. That was the stage, the reader will recall, when the disciples had come to speak of Jesus as the pre-existent 'Word' or 'Son' of God. This was an insight into Jesus – though, as we now know, it was, of course really a *hind-sight* or *resurrection-sight* into him – which John was particularly concerned with emphasising. Accordingly, we find that at the very outset, in the prologue, John leaves the reader in no doubt regarding Jesus' true origin and status:

> In the beginning was the Word:
> the Word was with God
> and the Word was God.
> … The Word was made flesh,
> he lived among us … (1: 14).

In order to proclaim loudly and clearly that Jesus was the

pre-existent 'Word' of God, John uses, throughout his version of the Good News, the device referred to, of presenting Jesus as one who, during his life, is conscious of 'preexisting', who, during his life, speaks as one who existed eternally and who, during his life, is generally, in Raymond E. Brown's phrases, 'omniscient' and 'emphatically knowing'. The result is, in Wilfrid Harrington's words, that

It is the majestic Word-made-flesh who strides through the pages of John (*The Jesus Story*, p 132).

In John, Jesus

… seems something of a sojourner from another world (p 21).

Of great relevance in our present context is the fact that the Jesus of the other gospels is not at all presented in this way. For, though these gospels also profess Jesus to be the Son of God, they do not, or at least do not in any clear way, present him as one who is conscious of existing eternally. The Jesus of John is, then, in very many ways different from the Jesus of the other three gospels. The Jesus of John is not, as Harrington puts it,

… so comfortably human as, say, the Jesus of Mark' (as above, p 132).

The difference between the Jesus of John and that of the other gospels can easily be illustrated. It emerges very clearly when, for example, we compare the Jesus who comes to his passion and death in the fourth gospel with the Jesus of the agony scene in Mark.

The Jesus of John, being conscious of 'pre-existence', is one who, on the night before he died, speaks calmly and serenely during supper of such matters as his intimate unity with the Father and of his own return 'in a little while':

Do not let your hearts be troubled.
Trust in God still, and trust in me.
There are many rooms in my Father's house;

if there were not, I should have told you.
I am going now to prepare a place for you,
and after I have gone and prepared you a place,
I shall return to take you with me;
so that where I am
you may be too.
You know the way to the place where I am going.
(Jn 14: 1ff)

The Jesus who comes to his last hour in John is described
well by Raymond E. Brown:

He is a Jesus conscious of his pre-existence. Through
death, therefore, he is returning to a state he has tempor-
arily left during his stay in this world ... (*A Crucified
Christ in Holy Week*, p 57).

There is little trace in any part of John's account of Jesus'
final night, of the Jesus of Mark in the agony scene:

They came to a small estate called Gethsemane, and Jesus
said to his disciples, 'Stay here while I pray'. Then he
took Peter and James and John with him. And a sudden
fear came over him, and great distress. And he said to
them, 'My soul is sorrowful to the point of death. Wait
here, and keep awake.' And going on a little further he
threw himself on the ground and prayed that, if it were
possible, this hour might pass him by. 'Abba (Father)!' he
said, 'Everything is possible for you. Take this cup away
from me. But let it be as you, not I, would have it ... (Mk
14: 32ff).

In John, in contrast to Mark, it is not Jesus who falls to the
ground in Gethsemane' but the soldiers who come to arrest
him. In John, in contrast to Mark, Jesus does not at all pray
that the 'cup' be taken from him and that, if possible, 'this
hour might pass him by': in John Jesus is, rather, content to
drink the cup that the Father has given him (18:11) and even
declines to pray that the Father should save him from this
hour:

What shall I say:
Father, save me from this hour?
But it was for this very reason that I have come to this
hour.
Father, glorify your name!
(12: 27; see R. E. Brown, as above, p 58).

John's Jesus in Christian consciousness
The second reason for taking John as my example is the
impact which this particular portrait of Jesus has had on
Christian consciousness. If we think about it, we will see
that it is John's picture of Jesus which has dominated in
Christian piety. Indeed, I think we will find it easy to agree
with Raymond E. Brown, when he says that this picture of
the man Jesus, speaking as one who existed before he was
born, is almost the only picture of Jesus with which many
people are familiar. A remark about John made by Brian O.
McDermott sums up well the way in which many people
understand Jesus:

> In John the notion begins to develop that Jesus said and
> did things for our instruction, *but not as part of his own de-*
> *veloping experience* (*Word Become Flesh*, pp 194-5, italics
> mine).

If this is how we see Jesus, then we will really find it difficult to take him seriously as one of us. And if we do not take
him seriously as one of us, then, as we know, we will never
understand how Christian faith really understands him as
'Son of God'. In that case, and in that sense, the gospels,
which are capable of being such a help in our understanding of Jesus will, in fact, have become a serious hindrance to
our doing so.

Telling a story with a purpose
But, the reader might well ask, can we ever really understand John's way of presenting Jesus, or indeed that of any
of the gospels? Can we at all hope to understand how John,
or any of the evangelists, can present Jesus as, for example,
speaking in a way in which he never did in fact speak?

Perhaps the best way of understanding this is to think of the gospels in terms of *story*, and to see an evangelist as one who is *telling a story with a purpose* – a way of understanding the gospels which Wilfrid Harrington, for example, suggests.

The gospels, it is important to remember, were written by believers for believers. They were written, then, for people who already knew the story of Jesus, and knew it as well as the evangelist himself did. But this did not mean that they did not need to hear it again. As Frank, a character in Brian Friel's play *Wonderful Tennessee*, says, when someone remarks that they all already know how the story which Trish is telling ends:

> So what? All we want of a story is to hear it again and again and again and again and again (*Act One, Scene Two*).

When a particular evangelist set out to tell the story of Jesus once again, he obviously did so with a very definite purpose – he set out, as Wilfrid Harrington says, to tell the story 'in *his* way'. *His* way was that which he thought would best bring out the particular faith-truth about Jesus which his community needed to hear at that particular time – for, we will recall, it was with the concerns and needs of his community in mind that he set out to tell the story in the first place.

Once we think of a gospel in terms of an evangelist telling a story, we have to think of the gospels as having *characterization and plot* – every story has these. Indeed, if we think about it, we shall see that it is, in fact, through characterization that storytellers brings the characters to life in their story, and that it is through characterization and plot that they make their point and, so, achieve their purpose in telling the story. In trying to understand Jesus as he is presented in a particular gospel, we might, then, as Wilfrid Harrington suggests, think of him as a 'character' in the evangelist's telling of the story.

We need to understand what a 'character' in a story is. As Harrington also reminds us, a 'character', in literary terms, is not quite the same as a person as he or she is known to people. In a story the teller does not just describe the person as he or she appears to others, from the outside, as it were. Rather, the storyteller interprets the person for us, helps us 'to get inside the character', and makes the person 'transparent' to us. In this way the storyteller creates a 'character' out of a person.

It is interesting – and important – to reflect on what the storyteller can achieve through characterization. He or she can give us insights into the person which an everyday meeting with the person would not, and could not, give. In this way, he or she can enable us to know the person even more fully than those who had met the person ever did. In Bernard Shaw's view the storyteller can – indeed ought to – help us even to understand the person more fully than the person actually understood himself or herself. Speaking of the function of the dramatist, Shaw says in the Preface to his *Saint Joan*:

> … it is the business of the stage to make its figures more intelligible to themselves than they would be in real life; for by no other means can they be made intelligible to the audience (*Saint Joan*, p 64).

It is interesting too to note how storytellers can make a person 'transparent' to us. They can do it in very obviously by telling us directly, in a straightforward way and in so many words, what their characters are really like. But they can do it also, indeed much more effectively, by means of *dramatisation*: they can do it, for example, as Harrington puts it,

> … by having them speak and act and by having others talk about them and speak to them (*The Jesus Story*, p 10).

Examples of characters from secular stories which come to mind here are the character Julius Caesar, or the character Brutus, of Shakespeare's play or the characters of Shaw's play *Saint Joan*. The Julius Caesar or the Brutus or the Joan of these plays obviously are not quite the same as the Julius Caesar or the Brutus or the Joan of history. Through characterization and dramatic plot, by making the characters speak and act and react, and by having others speak about them, the dramatists have, among other things, attempted to interpret these people for us and to give us insights into them which those who met them in the flesh did not have. Furthermore – and this is a very important point – in so far as the dramatists, as a result, for example, of insights gleaned from centuries of research and reflection, might really have understood these people, they would then have succeeded in enabling us to understand them in a way that the people who met them could never have understood them. So, of his presentation of the characters Cauchon, Lemaître (the Inquisator), and Warwick in *Saint Joan*, Shaw says:

> ... as far as I can gather from the available documentation, and from such powers of divination as I possess, the things I represent these three exponents of the drama as saying are the things they actually would have said if they had known what they were really doing (*Saint Joan*, p 65).

With regard to the gospels, Wilfrid Harrington says:

> This distinction between 'character' and 'person' is very important. Jesus of Nazareth was a thoroughly historical person. He was a first-century Palestinian Jew who carried out what – he was convinced – was a God-given mission to his people. He was rejected, and was condemned and executed by an alliance of Jewish religious and Roman political authorities. The 'character' Jesus of the gospels is this Jesus now viewed through Christian eyes, seen through the prism of resurrection-faith (as above, pp 10-11).

Christians, of course, believe that the resurrection-faith gives the *true* insight into who Jesus really was. Accordingly, they believe that the 'character' Jesus in a particular gospel is not simply the figment of the particular evangelist's imagination but actually brings out an aspect of the full truth about Jesus. In that way, as Harrington also says:

> The gospels, in which Jesus is a literary character, make him known to us more profoundly than he, as a person, was in fact known to his contemporaries (as above, p 10).

* * *

Once we begin to see the gospels as the unique documents which they are, inevitably many questions arise in our minds, particularly regarding 'inspiration', the truth of the gospels, and our knowledge of Jesus as he lived in history. We cannot deal with these questions here – the focus in this book is on the 'Incarnation' rather than the gospels. The interested reader will, no doubt, pursue such questions elsewhere, guided, perhaps, by the references given in the notes to this chapter and to the previous one. Some points in this connection will also be made in Appendix One. What concerns us here is the importance of thinking of Jesus as a real human being. In this connection, only one main point is being made about the gospels: whenever we set out to talk about Jesus *as he lived in history*, we need to be very careful in our use of these documents. Since the gospels do not attempt to report in a straightforward and 'objective' way what Jesus had said and done, obviously, we may not take – or quote – the words of the gospels as always necessarily reporting historical facts.

In this connection there is one point in particular which can be helpful to remember. We shall see in the next chapter that there are certain gospel passages which attribute human limitations and weaknesses to Jesus – for example, there are the passages in Mark and Matthew which present him as saying the equivalent of 'I don't know this; nobody does except the Father' (Mk 13:32; Mt 24:34). In view of the

post-resurrection perspective from which Jesus is understood and presented in the gospels, such passages are most
likely to represent Jesus as he was actually known and experienced during his life. This is a point which should help
the reader to understand the use of passages from the gospels in the chapters which follow.

The ordinariness of Jesus

CHAPTER FOUR

His own person or divine puppet?

It is one thing to *say* that Jesus was 'truly human'. It is another to be convinced of this and really to mean it. As I have said, it is not at the level of creed that our reluctance to think of Jesus as a real human being is likely to manifest itself today – at this level there is 'a profound orthodoxy'. It begins to emerge, rather, only when the details of our picture of Jesus begin to become clear. If we are to be sure that we really do see Jesus as a human being, we need to reflect on his life in some detailed way. This section on *The Ordinariness of Jesus* will focus on certain features of human life and will emphasise that these were in fact characteristics of his life too. The features chosen are ones which, in my experience, people do not usually associate with Jesus, and which, in fact, they are often afraid to associate with him. Any ambivalence which might still be lurking in the reader's mind regarding Jesus *really* being a real human being should in this way be uncovered.

Jesus' attitude before God

The first point on which it is important to reflect, it seems to me, is how Jesus saw himself in relation to God. Did this human being, the carpenter from Nazareth, stand before God in an attitude of creatureliness before his Creator or in some other relationship?

The answer which immediately occurs to the Christian is that Jesus stood before God as the Son in whom the Father is well pleased, to use the language of the baptism and transfiguration stories. And this, of course, is the correct Christian answer. Christians, believing as they do that Jesus was uniquely the Son of God, naturally believe that he stood before God in this unique relationship.

But while the man, Jesus, stood before God as the Son in whom the Father was well pleased, it is of the greatest importance to remember that the Jesus who stood before God in this way, was nonetheless a human being, a carpenter from Nazareth. As such, he stood before God 'in utter creatureliness'. To say otherwise would surely be equivalent to saying that he was not really a human being at all: human beings are, after all, creatures.

It was because Jesus stood before God in a creaturely way that the scriptures, including the gospels, can present him as acting as only a creature can before God.

It is why they can present him as, for example, *praying to God*. Here the agony scene immediately comes to mind (Mk 14: 32ff; Mt 26:36; Lk 22:39ff). But there is also the passage in Mark which says:

> In the morning, long before dawn, he got up and left the house, and went off to a lonely place and prayed there (1: 35; Lk 4:42).

There is the passage in Luke which says:

> … he spent the whole night in prayer to God (6: 12).

And there is the passage where Matthew says:

> After sending the crowds away he went up into the hills by himself to pray (14: 23).

There are also, of course, the many occasions on which it is said that:

> … he gave thanks (e.g. Mt 15: 36; Lk 22: 19).

It is because of his creatureliness that Jesus could also have *felt abandoned by God*, and, so, could be presented as crying out on the cross the line from psalm 22:

> My God, my God, why have you deserted me? (Mk 15:34; Mt 27: 46).

It is the fact of his sense of creatureliness before God that alone explains *his attitude towards the Father's will*. We will notice that whenever in the gospels he is confronted with the Father's will (as in the agony scene), he is presented as experiencing it as authoritative, making demands on him, and as something which he ought to obey (Mk 14: 32ff; Mt 26:36; Lk 22:39ff). The reason is that though it was the will of the One he called 'Father', it was, nonetheless, the will of the One who gave him his being in the first place and who continued to give it to him – it was the will of his *Creator*.

Jesus: Free before God

In trying to think of Jesus as a real human being it can be helpful also to reflect further on the fact that Jesus was *free* before God. To say that Jesus was not really free would, of course, be the same as saying that he was not really human. So it was that when, in the 7th century, Sergius I, Patriarch of Constantinople, said that the human will of Jesus was absorbed by and was lost in the divine will, the Sixth Council of Constantinople declared that Jesus, being truly human, had his own human will.

It is not necessary here to discuss in any detailed way the notion of human 'freedom'. Being one of the basic characteristics of the human creature, it is not a simple matter. In the present context it will help to draw attention to just two characteristics of earthly freedom and their implications for understanding Jesus.

Jesus: Author of his own script

There is nobody today of whom I know who sets out to deny, in so many words, that Jesus was free before God. There are, however, many who, perhaps without being fully aware of this, actually think of him as not being really free. For there are many who see Jesus as one who, throughout his life, followed, almost blindly, a course of action laid out for him by God. They recall many passages from the gospels which say 'as it was written' or 'this was to fulfil the prophecy', and they interpret these passages as though they were referring to a script written by God for Jesus' life, and in the writing of which Jesus himself had no part. They altogether forget, or ignore, the 'hindsight' perspective from which the gospels were written and the dramatic way in which the Jesus-story is related. They do not see Jesus, then, as being a free man, but rather as that 'puppet on strings' of which Karl Rahner speaks.

It is true, of course, that, for all of us, the direction of our lives is to some extent shaped by forces outside our control. It is shaped, for example, by the time in history and the place in the world in which we are born, by who our parents were, by our gender, our genes, our upbringing and so on. But, allowing for all this, we still have, to some extent at least, the shaping of our destinies in our own hands. The fact is that all through our lives we find ourselves standing, in freedom, before various possible courses of action, and choosing between these: we choose, for example, what career to follow, whether to marry or not to marry, whether to marry this person or another. According as we make these free choices, we determine, to that extent, what course our life takes from there. In that way we ourselves make and shape the person we become and so we are, at least in that sense of the phrase, 'self-made' people. In so far as we do all this freely, we are responsible for who and what we are. It is we ourselves, then, who, within the limits referred to above, freely write our own script for our own lives.

As regards Jesus, Christians obviously are convinced that God was deeply and intimately involved in his life from its inception to its passing on to newness of life in the resurrection. However, once we say that Jesus was 'truly human', then we may not think of God's involvement in his life as in anyway taking away from his freedom. How we might explain this is another matter – it is a matter which will arise later in the broader context of the relation between the

divine and human in Jesus. But, however we might explain
it, we must acknowledge it to be a fact.

Because the divine presence and action in Jesus did not remove his freedom, the pattern of his life was basically the
same as ours. Jesus, just as much as we, was frequently
faced with various possible courses of action. He, just as
much as we, was frequently choosing freely between the
possibilities which lay before him, whether it was a matter
of what career to follow, or, later, of how best and most
effectively to exercise his ministry – whether, for example,
to accept the offer to be made king or to chose the more
lonely road of the prophet, or, later still, of whether or not to
avoid confrontation. Jesus had, then, the making of himself
and the shaping of his destiny in his own hands in the same
general way that we all have. Accordingly, it was *he himself*
who was responsible for the course which his life took and
for the person he became. It was *he himself* who decided
freely to leave carpentry and become a preacher or rabbi. It
was *he himself* who freely chose to opt particularly for the
poor and the outcast. It was *he himself* who freely decided to
reject the offer to become king. It was *he himself* who freely
chose to confront the religious authorities. It was *he himself*
who chose to accept the chalice of death and suffering. Since
Jesus wrote his own script for his life, at least as much as we
write our script for our lives, he was far from being a divine
'puppet'; he was, indeed, very much 'his own person'.

Jesus and temptation

The second implication of Jesus' freedom which is worth
thinking about here is that Jesus could be, and was, tempted. Theologically speaking, to be tempted means to be
attracted to chose what one knows in one's heart would not
be the right thing to choose – generally, when we talk about
temptation we seem to talk about temptation to do wrong
rather than to do right. To be tempted is, then, to be attracted
to make an immoral choice – it is to be attracted to be im-

moral. And it is to be really attracted to this, for if there is no real attraction, there is no real temptation.

It is interesting that the gospels, though written after Jesus was recognised to be Son and Lord, make no bones whatsoever about presenting him as being open to temptation. The accounts of the temptations after forty days in the wilderness immediately come to mind. It is not our task here to deal in a detailed way with these accounts except to suggest, with scholars, that they are perhaps best understood as representing, in a dramatic and symbolic way, the temptations to which Jesus was subjected throughout his whole life. What concerns us here is not the precise nature of these temptations, but the fact that three of the gospels, Mark, Matthew and Luke, do not hesitate to present Jesus as being, from the very outset of his ministry, one who was open to temptation.

Of course it is not only in these stories that the gospels present Jesus as being subjected to temptation. Peter too is presented as tempting him by trying to dissuade him from going up to Jerusalem, a journey which would involve that fatal confrontation with the religious authorities. The strength of this temptation comes out in the reply attributed to Jesus:

Get behind me, Satan! (Mk 8: 33; cf Mt 16: 23)

In the gospel according to Mark, temptation seems also to have come to Jesus even from his own family: these, it would appear, had serious reservations and doubts about his activities:

He went home again, and once more such a crowd collected that they could not even have a meal. When his relatives heard of this, they set out to take charge of him, convinced he was out of his mind (3: 20-21).

With regard to being subjected to temptation, the Letter to the Hebrews does not hesitate to put Jesus on the very same level as the rest of us when it says:

For it is not as if we had a high priest who was incapable of feeling our weaknesses with us; but we have one who has been tempted in every way that we are, though he is without sin (4: 15).

'... though he is without sin'

The purpose of this chapter is not to deal with the uniqueness of Jesus: its aim is rather to emphasise that, however unique he was, he was a humble human being. However, the phrase 'without sin' used in the above passage from Hebrews, though it does refer to the uniqueness of Jesus, requires some comment at this point. This is because, in my experience, this phrase can actually be an obstacle to people thinking of Jesus as being really human: 'After all', it has often been said to me, `to err is human, and, so, to sin is human. If Jesus did not sin, he was not really human at all'.

The problem here is a mistaken idea of what 'without sin' means. Ultimately, of course, it is a mistaken idea of what 'sin' means.

We might begin by saying what sin is not. Sin is not the same as the experience of human weakness – thus the gospels of Mark and Matthew can present Jesus as saying

... the flesh is weak (Mk 14: 38; Mt 26: 42).

Nor is sin the same as the immaturity of the child. Maturity means ripeness. But growing to ripeness or maturity, especially to moral ripeness and maturity, is a normal and natural part of the process of human growth. So Luke does not hesitate to speak of Jesus as growing, not just physically, but (in a reference to Samuel of old), 'to maturity' (2: 40). He even speaks of Jesus as increasing

... in wisdom, in stature, and in favour with God and people (2: 52).

I find it interesting that though this is a text with which most people are familiar, the idea of Jesus growing in favour with God often seems somehow new to many.

Sin, we should remember, is a very specific concept. It has to do with moral living – or, rather, with the absence of this. It occurs when, and only when, a person freely chooses what he or she knows should not, in this situation, be chosen. Sin, then, involves free choice and knowledge.

To say that Jesus was 'without sin' cannot, then, be the same as saying that he was never young and never experienced the immaturity that necessarily goes with being young – it cannot mean, therefore, that he was never really young (an understanding of Jesus which would, I imagine, be another form of the 'phantomism' referred to in the first chapter). Nor is it even necessarily the same as saying that he never, throughout his whole life, erred or made a mistake. Strictly speaking, it is to say only that he never *freely* chose what he *knew* to be contrary to the Father's will and, so, that he was never immoral.

To err, then, may be human. But to sin is not the same as to err. To sin, properly understood, is to decide, knowingly and freely, to go off-target in human living – as the Greek word *hamartia* ('missing the mark'), one of the main biblical words for sin, suggests. Far, then, from being a humanizing factor in life, sin is, in fact, a de-humanizing factor. So, contrary to what seems to be often thought, to say that Jesus was 'without sin' is not at all to imply that he was not human. Rather, it is to say that, being always and consistently a moral person, he was, therefore, always and consistently *authentically* human. Once we understand sin in this way, we will immediately understand why Christians, believing as they do that in Jesus God was present in human history in a definitive way, believe that Jesus was actually 'without sin', and why they even believe that it would have been altogether inconceivable for him to have sinned. A point worth mentioning, if only in passing here, is that his 'sin-lessness' did not at all separate Jesus from sinners. The opposite, rather was the case: judging by the way Jesus is presented in the gospels, and in Christian preaching generally, as the friend of sinners, even dining with them, his 'sin-lessness' drew him towards sinners and sinners towards him. What this says about the God who Christians believe was present in Jesus offers food for considerable thought and reflection.

Talking about the 'sinlessness' of Jesus is, then, really only a rather negative way of talking about his consistently moral and virtuous living. We should not think of the 'sinlessness' of Jesus as being merely the innocence of the child. Virtue and childlike innocence, I find, are often confused with each other – so much so, indeed, that the innocent child is some-times put forward as the model of virtue. Innocence has to do with 'guilelessness' or 'ignorance of evil' (in its literal sense, the word suggests simply 'harmlessness'). Innocence is a characteristic of every infant and is, therefore, some-thing in which knowledge and free choice do not necessarily play any part at all. In itself, therefore, it does not at all con-stitute truly moral living. In virtue, however, knowledge and free choice are essential elements, for virtue has to do with moral living. The 'sinlessness' of Jesus, then, is not at all the same as the nice ready-made innocence of the child: it is not, in John Macquarrie's phrase, 'a merely negative "dreaming innocence"'. 'Sinlessness' refers rather to the rugged, hard-won virtue of the mature moral person.

Since the question of the 'sinlessness' of Jesus arises here only in passing, it is not our task to try to explain this unique aspect of Jesus. However we explain the fact of Jesus' being 'without sin', and even the inconceivability of his sin-ning, it would seem to me at least that we may not do so by saying that Jesus was not free to sin or to act immorally. To say that Jesus was not free to be immoral would seem to me to be the equivalent of saying that he was not moral at all. In this earthly situation at least, one can be moral only through freely choosing to do what one knows to be right. And one can freely choose what one knows to be right, only if one can also freely choose not to do it – that is, only if one can freely choose to do what one knows to be wrong. To say that Jesus was not free to be immoral would seem to me, then, really to amount to saying that he was not free to be moral. But if he was not free to be moral was he actually moral at all? He might, in that situation, be said to be 'innocent', but he could hardly be said to be moral.

* * *

There is far more to professing that Jesus was 'truly human' than often meets the eye. In professing this, if we take seriously the Christian community's insistence that Jesus had human freedom, we must also be saying, with Karl Rahner, that Jesus

... possesses a genuine, spontaneous, free, spiritual, active centre, a human selfconsciousness ...

which, as creaturely, faces God

in a genuinely human attitude of adoration, obedience, a most radical sense of creaturehood (*Theological Investigations*, vol 1, p 158).

We are saying, in the words of Luke, that Jesus too had to grow

... in stature and in favour with God and people (2: 52).

CHAPTER FIVE

'How much did Jesus know?'

'How much did Jesus know? Did he know he was God?' These are questions which, in my experience, are asked sooner or later – sooner rather than later – in every group in which Jesus is discussed. And they always seem to be asked in a purely inquisitive sort of way – as though 'just as a matter of interest'. The question of the knowledge of Jesus is, however, much more than a matter of curiosity. It is, in fact, a very good way of asking how really human Jesus was. And our views on it are a very good test of whether or not we really regard Jesus as human at all. The topic of the knowledge of Jesus requires to be discussed here at some length.

That a Christian today should ask 'Did Jesus know he was God?' is understandable since most Christians today think of Jesus first of all as 'a divine person' and remember him as he is portrayed in John. Understandable as the question is, we should, not, however, allow its implications at least to escape us. What is really being asked is, of course: 'Did the carpenter from Nazareth know he was God?'

Awareness of his 'divine Sonship'

We need to introduce the discussion of the knowledge of Jesus by referring to the Christian conviction regarding the 'divine Sonship' of Jesus. What exactly this conviction is, is not being discussed at this point. In general terms – and admittedly only in very general terms – the 'divine Sonship' refers to the Christian conviction that God was active and present in Jesus in a unique, indeed in a decisive and definitive, way.

It can easily be seen, I think, that anyone who believes in such a unique involvement of God in Jesus must see it as having a most profound effect on him, affecting particularly his consciousness. To say that Jesus himself was not in any way conscious of God's special presence in him would imply that God, in becoming involved in Jesus, ignored that which is specifically human in him, his intellect. It would be to imply that God treated Jesus in a subhuman way. This, of course, would be unthinkable, and it is not, as we know, how the Christian community understands God to be present in Jesus. For this reason alone, we must say that if God was always present to Jesus in a unique way, then Jesus in his consciousness was also always present to God in a uniquely profound and intimate way. We must say, in other words, that Jesus was, *in some way or other*, conscious of his identity or, in Christian terms, of his 'divine Sonship'. This conclusion is in line with the way in which all the gospels consistently portray Jesus as being in continual and deep communion with God – as Jesus must in fact have been during his life.

We must say too that if, as Christians believe, Jesus had a unique, indeed a definitive, role in God's plan, then he must also have been aware of this in some way: it would be rather difficult to think of Jesus as exercising in any effective way a role which he did not know was his! We cannot, then, think of Jesus as seeing himself as, for example, just one other prophet in the long line of prophets who had appeared throughout the history of Israel. We have to think of him rather as being, in some way, deeply conscious of the defin–itive mission which Christians believe was his. This too is a conclusion which would be in line with the way the gospels present Jesus: they present him as speaking and acting with great divinely-given authority. So, in Matthew, for exam-ple, he is presented as speaking with greater authority than even Moses:

You have learnt how it was said to our ancestors: You

must not kill ... But *I* say this to you ... (Mt 5: 21-22 and
following verses; italics mine).

The evidence is that Jesus did actually speak and act during
his life with such a sure sense of divinely given authority.

But limited in knowledge

All this might easily lead one to the conclusion that Jesus
had, therefore, access to unlimited knowledge. It did in fact
lead people to this conclusion. So, even the relatively recent
standard textbooks of theology presented Jesus as knowing,
to quote from one of these,

> ... everything that exists, that did exist and that will exist;
> everything that was done or said or thought by anyone
> (G. Van Noort, *De Verbo Incarnato*, p 74, par 110).

This, of course, is a conclusion which might also seem to be
supported by the many gospel passages which attribute
extraordinary knowledge to Jesus. He is presented, for example, as having knowledge of what people were thinking
inwardly:

> ... Jesus knew them all and did not trust himself to them;
> he never needed evidence about any man; he could tell
> what a man had in him (Jn 2: 24-25; see also Mk 2: 6-8; 9:
> 33-34; Lk 9: 46-47; Jn 16: 19, 30).

He is presented as having a knowledge of what was going
to happen elsewhere:

> So he sent two of his disciples, saying to them, 'Go into the
> city and you will meet a man carrying a pitcher of water.
> Follow him, and say to the owner of the house which he
> enters, "The Master says: Where is my dining room in
> which I can eat the passover with my disciples?" He will
> show you a large upper room furnished with couches, all
> prepared. Make the preparations for us there.' The disci-
> ples set out and went to the city and found everything as
> he had told them ... (Mk 14:13-16; see also Mk 11: 2ff; Mt
> 17: 24-27; Lk 22: 10).

He is presented also as having a detailed knowledge of the future, in particular of his own final destiny. This is not just true of John which portrayed Jesus as being conscious, during his life, of 'pre-existence'; even in Mark, for example, Jesus is presented as giving beforehand a very detailed account of his own passion:

> Now we are going up to Jerusalem, and the Son of Man is about to be handed over to the chief priests and the scribes. They will condemn him to death and will hand him over to the pagans, who will mock him and spit at him and scourge him and put him to death; and after three days he will rise again (10: 33-34; *cf* Mt 20: 18-19).

The conclusion that Jesus had unlimited, or almost unlimited, knowledge might, indeed, seem to have a scriptural foundation.

The question of the knowledge of Jesus in scripture will be discussed later in this chapter. It can be said at this point, however, that the conclusion that Jesus had access to unlimited, or almost unlimited, knowledge is one which simply cannot be accepted and cannot, therefore, really be solidly based in scripture. It is a conclusion which cannot be accepted because if we accept that Jesus had access to this kind of knowledge, then we have let go of the idea that he really was a human being – we have let go, not just of the Jesus of history, the carpenter from Nazareth, but also of the *truly human* Christ of the faith of the Church.

I say this for three reasons in particular. They arise from even an elementary reflection on what is necessarily entailed in living a mature human life.

1. First we might reflect on the part which *growing in knowledge* plays in human life. Growing in knowledge – in knowledge of ourselves, of others, and of the world around us – is an essential feature of what we know as mature human living. Having new experiences, meeting new people, coming up against the unexpected, being surprised and disappoint-

ed, encountering new ideas, struggling to learn and to understand, to assimilate and integrate what is learned, is an essential part of living a mature human life. It would indeed be interesting for the reader to consider each of these in turn and try to remove them from his or her own life, and then try to imagine what of his or her experience of adult living would be left! This, it might be said in passing, is not to pass any judgement whatsoever on the human quality, in God's eyes, of the lives of those who, due to some handicap, are unable to grow and mature as 'normal' human beings. It is, however, to acknowledge the fact that Jesus is not believed to have suffered such a handicap but is thought of as being, among other things, a model of mature, adult human living.

Now if Jesus, in virtue of his presence to God, had a knowledge of '... everything that exists, that did exist and that will exist; everything that was done or said or thought by anyone', how could he be said to have grown in knowledge at all? How could he be said to have had new experiences – for example, how could he be said to have experienced surprise or disappointment? And if he had not experienced these aspects of human living and had not been immersed in our slow human struggle to learn and to understand, how could he be said to have lived a mature human life? Here it ought to be said that the theology textbooks referred to above also acknowledged that since Jesus was truly human, he had to have grown in knowledge – strange though this may seem in view of the passage from G. Van Noort which has been quoted. So, they found it necessary to try to show how Jesus could both increase in knowledge in the normal human way and at the same time have access to unlimited knowledge – a rather difficult task, the reader will admit. Their efforts to resolve this problem need not concern us here as they belong now to the history of theology. What is of interest to us here is that theology has always recognised the fact that Jesus, being human, had to grow in knowledge.

2. As I have pointed out in the previous chapter, and as we know anyway from our experience of living, the element of having *to make choices* plays an important role in our lives. Having to choose between different courses of action which lie open before us, having to ponder before we choose, having to pray and to agonize over choices, having to live with the sometimes painful, sometimes joyful, consequences of our choices, and having to take responsibility for the person we become as a result of our free choices, is, we all know, the very stuff of which mature human living is made. Here again it would be interesting for the reader to reflect on the important place which all of this has in his or her own life.

A question which arises with regard to Jesus, therefore, is how could he have experienced all – or indeed any – of this, if he always (even as an infant) knew beforehand exactly what choice he was going to make and where exactly each choice was going to lead him – if, in other words, he always had before his eyes God's script for his life and saw this in clear detail? But if Jesus did not experience this feature of human living, in what sense could he be said to have experienced human living at all?

Lack of knowledge, it should be noted here, is not, when we think about it, a purely negative factor in human life. It has the positive value of enabling us to exercise, in our present situation, our greatest faculty, freedom. For in enabling us to move thoughtfully into the darkness of the future, it is, as Karl Rahner says,

> ... the dark ground of freedom itself and ... the condition making it possible' (*Theological Investigations*, vol 5, p 202).

Seen in this way, ignorance, in our present situation at least, is

> ... more perfect for this exercise of freedom than knowledge which would suspend this exercise (as above).

To attribute to Jesus a lack of knowledge is not at all, then, to attribute some human imperfection to him, even though it was often seen in this way. On the contrary, it is only to assert that it was possible for him to live a real mature human life.

3. A third reason why we cannot think of Jesus as having unlimited, or almost unlimited, knowledge, becomes clear when we reflect, even briefly, on the *authenticity* of Jesus' relationship with the people of his time. Being authentic with people, being straight, honest and open with them is, surely, a basic human virtue. Common respect for people demands it. Now if Jesus had the almost unlimited knowledge so often attributed to him, in what sense was he authentic with people? Presumably he asked questions as a child – children always do. Scripture, as I shall note again later, does not hesitate to present him as asking questions as an adult: 'Where have they laid him (Lazarus)?', 'Who was it who touched me?', etc. But in what sense could these have been real questions if the person who asked them already knew the answers? And if Jesus already knew the answers, in what sense was he being real and authentic with people in asking them questions at all? Furthermore, in what sense could he have been authentic with people if he withheld knowledge from them – if, for example, he, the great friend of the down-trodden, and the man of great compassion, knew of modern technological developments and yet watched people struggle with primitive working methods and living conditions? A life of pretence and insincerity and inauthenticity could hardly be a role-model for human living. It is difficult (to put it mildly) to see how it could be attributed to the one who is believed to be the unique Son of God on earth – that is, of course, unless we are prepared to see this life as not a *real* human life at all, but as just a-going-through-the-motions of living! But, in that case we would be thinking of Jesus, not at all as the real human being which he was, but as a human *mask* put on by God just to make the divine Self visible.

'... he increased in wisdom ... ' (Lk 2: 52)

So far, I have been saying what, in terms of knowledge, could not have been true of Jesus. It is now necessary to speak of his knowledge in more positive terms and to say what must have been true of him.

When we come to do this we need, of course, to remember how impossible a task it is to talk in any detailed way about Jesus' knowledge. In talking about Jesus, we are, after all, talking about one who, on any reckoning, was one of the most influential and insightful figures in human history, and who, in the Christian view, was in a unique way aware of, and attuned to, the divine presence in himself and in life. The inner mystery of the mind of this man is, then, something we cannot hope to fathom. The impossibility of penetrating the inner mind of Jesus will be particularly clear to anyone who is at all familiar with the lives and experiences and insights of the great mystics or even with the life and experiences and insights of, for example, such a remarkably perceptive person of modern times as Carl G. Jung. In speaking in positive terms about the consciousness of this unique and most creative of people, we can, then, only make some points of a very general nature. For our present purposes, such general points are all that need to be made.

Allowing for Jesus' profound awareness of, and his deep communion with, God, and for the fact that he was a man of extraordinary perceptiveness and insight, we can – indeed must – say that the following two characteristics of all earthly knowledge were characteristics of his knowledge too: we can and must say this of Jesus if we are to think of him as a real human being.

1. Gradually acquired
We can and must say, first of all, that whatever factual knowledge Jesus had of the world around him, was *acquired gradually*. Like ourselves, to use words from Luke, 'he increased in wisdom' (2: 52); like ourselves, (at our best), he

was always passing from ignorance (if that word is not understood in its pejorative sense) to knowledge; like ourselves, he came to know today what he did not know yesterday.

This means, for example, that Jesus shared with us the sometimes painful, sometimes exciting, movement into the darkness of the future. In particular, like ourselves, he faced the darkness of death, 'this trackless dark', as Karl Rahner has referred to it. This is so, despite the passage from the gospels quoted above in which Jesus is presented as foretelling his resurrection 'after three days'. This passage, like all gospel passages, needs to be understood in the light of what the author was really teaching about Jesus when he put these words into his mouth.

Regarding Jesus' attitude towards his violent death, many Christians, I find, have very mistaken and, indeed, unacceptable ideas. They think of him as willing this particular death, as though he had a 'death-wish'. Jesus, of course, would have been well aware of the dark power of evil and of the fate of the prophets before him. However, Jesus would, surely, have wished, and dearly hoped, that even his opponents would have a change of heart, would become open to his message and, so, would come to accept both it and him. His violent death came because people who had the power to have him put to death were threatened by him, by what he said and by what he did and by his freedom, and, so, wanted to dispose of him. Jesus accepted this death because the only alternative would have been to act against his convictions and, so, to be untrue to himself, to people and, ultimately, to God. We should think of him, then, not so much as willing his violent death, but as freely accepting it. His attitude to it is summed up in the agony prayer:

'Father', he said, 'if you are willing, take this cup away from me. Nevertheless, let your will be done, not mine' (Lk 22: 42).

As to his emotional reactions in the face of his coming death, we are given some insight into these in the account of the agony in Mark, quoted already in Chapter Three, where we read of 'a sudden fear' and 'great distress' coming over Jesus, of Jesus being sorrowful 'to the point of death', and throwing himself on the ground as he prayed (Mk 14: 32ff).

This 'trackless dark' which death is for all of us may well indeed have been more trackless for Jesus than for us: we, at least, have heard of Jesus' death-leading-to-resurrection, but this was something for which Jesus himself could only hope. Jesus faced 'this trackless dark' of death in the way he had always faced the darkness of the future – in faith, hope, and love. A description of the faith-full attitude with which we might think of Jesus facing his death is offered by Karl Rahner:

> In the unity of ... faith, hope, and love, Jesus surrendered himself in his death unconditionally to the absolute mystery that he called his Father, into whose hands he committed his existence, when in the night of his death and God-forsakenness he was deprived of everything that is otherwise regarded as the content of a human existence: life, honour, acceptance in earthly and religious fellowship, and so on. In the concreteness of his death it becomes only too clear that everything fell away from him, even the perceptible security of the closeness of God's love, and in this trackless dark there prevailed silently only the mystery that ... has no name and to which he nevertheless calmly surrendered himself as to eternal love and not to the hell of futility. (*Theological Investigations*, vol 18, p 165).

2. Historically and culturally conditioned

We can and must say, secondly, that Jesus' knowledge was conditioned by the historical and cultural situation in which he lived. Allowing once again for the hiddenness of what went on in the mysterious depths of Jesus' psyche, we must still say that his knowledge, like ours, was limited by, for example, the places he visited and knew of, the people he came into contact with and was influenced by, and the ideas he encountered. In this respect Jesus was, indeed, a man of his time.

This does not mean that he was not also ahead of his time. Like any remarkably perceptive and insightful key-person in history – indeed, in a faith-view, more than anyone else in history – Jesus, while being a person of his time, was also ahead of it. Raymond E. Brown, for example, referring to the findings of biblical scholarship, makes the point that

> ... there is an important area where the teaching of Jesus was unique, outdistancing the ideas of his time – the area of his own mission and the proclamation of the Kingdom of God (*Jesus God and Man*, p 59).

However, true as this is, it is also true that in his knowledge and understanding of the world around him, Jesus was, on the whole, limited and conditioned by the historical, geographical and cultural situation in which he lived and died.

Arising from this, there are three points in particular on which the reader might find it interesting and helpful to reflect.

The first has to do with how Jesus might have understood himself, and how he might have expressed, even for himself, his role in God's plan. Jesus was a Jew of the first century and, so, thought in the categories and spoke the language of the first century Jewish world. Not belonging to the Hellenistic world of later centuries, he would not have had available to him the concepts and the language of this world. Consequently we can hardly think of him as having used such language and concepts. In this context it is particularly interesting and important to note that Jesus himself would not have thought or talked about his own relationship with God in the terms in which later theology was, for the most part at least, to talk about this, that is, in terms of 'nature' (*physis*) and 'person' (*hypostasis*). There can be little doubt that when the Council of Chalcedon, for example, spoke about Jesus in these terms it expressed truths about him which needed to be expressed in this way at the time. It should not be forgotten, however, that the terms used were not ones with which Jesus himself would have been familiar. If we wish to have any idea of how Jesus himself might have understood and spoke about himself, we need to have a knowledge of his own Jewish background and, in particular, of the Jewish scriptures.

The second point has to do with drawing conclusions from the practice of Jesus himself as to what the Church might or might not do in later centuries. From what has been said about the knowledge of Jesus, it ought to be clear that it would be wrong to think of him, or to talk about him, as if he foresaw clearly every situation in the years ahead – as far as we today are concerned, 2,000 years ahead. Even allowing for the unique insight and perception which must have been his, it would still be foolish to think of him as having been simply outside or above history, as viewing all future situations, and as making detailed plans for these. It would be foolish to think of Jesus in that way because it would be impossible to think of any human being as seeing all the millennia ahead. This is not to imply that nothing at all can be said to have been, in theological language, 'instituted by Christ' and, so, to be of 'divine institution'. But in view of Jesus' own immersion in history and the limited nature of his knowledge, these are, obviously, very complex concepts. They are ones with which we cannot, and need not, deal here, though they have been examined in a detailed and scholarly way by theologians. Only one point needs to be made here, that is, to point to the obvious naïvety of the *simple* argument: 'Jesus did not order matters in this way, therefore the Church never can.'

The third point on which the reader might find it interesting to reflect has to do with the roles of Mary and Joseph in the formation and upbringing of Jesus. If we were to see Jesus as almost all-knowing, then, obviously, we would find it very difficult to assign any real role here to these – the phantomism latent in our thinking about Jesus himself would have serious implications for our understanding of their roles too. For, at least in terms of the *upbringing* of Jesus, they would have had to contribute little or nothing and, so, in this respect their parental roles would be reduced to mere appearances. Once we realise, however, that Jesus, like other human beings, was very dependent for his formation on the influences around him, particularly, of course, on the home influence, we can see that we need to think, much more deeply perhaps than we have been accustomed to doing, about the major influence which Mary and Joseph could have had in the formation of the mind and the heart of this man who so influenced human history. This is not to say that Jesus was totally dependent on these influences: no human being is simply the product of his or her environment. But it is to say that a characteristic of God's involvement in human affairs which we have already encountered appears here again. God's presence in Jesus himself did not prevent Jesus from being one hundred per cent a human being. God's involvement in the writing of the Bible did not prevent the human authors from being one hundred per cent 'true authors'. In the same way God's involvement in the formation and education of the mind and outlook of Jesus did not have to override, or take away from, or in any way diminish, the parental roles of Mary and Joseph in that process. In the formation and education of Jesus, they were capable of exercising true and full parental roles. This characteristic of God's involvement in human affairs, its *creative* character, is a most important matter and one to which I shall return in chapter eleven: an understanding of it will, I believe, prove to be crucial to our understanding of the relationship between the divine and human in Jesus.

The knowledge of Jesus in the gospels

What, then, is to be said about the impression that the gospels attribute to Jesus extraordinary knowledge, even a clear knowledge of the future? Obviously a detailed study of the knowledge of Jesus as portrayed in the gospels is not possible here. Very many such studies do, of course, exist and might be consulted by the reader – a very accessible one is that of Raymond E. Brown in his book *Jesus God and Man*. For our purposes I think it is enough to make just three points. They are very general, but very important points.

The first echoes what has been said above. It is that anyone who recognises the influence which Jesus has had on history ought not to be at all surprised to find him portrayed as a man of extraordinary insight and perception. In fact, had he not been such a man, it would be rather difficult to account for his impact on history. A Christian in particular, who believes that Jesus was attuned, in an unequalled way, to the divine presence in the world, will not be surprised at this.

The second is that the gospels' portrayal of the knowledge of Jesus is not at all as simple and as straightforward as people often think. The gospel-passages which attribute to Jesus extraordinary knowledge – interestingly and, I believe, significantly – are the ones which have become imprinted in peoples' minds. As a result, the impression is often formed that the gospels portray Jesus as one who was simply 'all-knowing'. However, texts which present Jesus as having extraordinary knowledge do not tell the whole story. It is important to know that the same gospels also present Jesus as one who had limited knowledge.

Biblical scholars draw our attention, for example, to texts which describe Jesus as *asking questions* : 'How many loaves have you?' (Mk 6: 38; 8: 5); 'Who touched me?' (*cf* Mk 5: 30-33); 'Where have you put him?' (Jn 11: 34)

There is the well known childhood story in Luke in which

Jesus as a boy is portrayed as being *anxious to learn* from those older and more learned than himself:

> Three days later, they found him in the Temple, sitting among the doctors, listening to them and asking them questions; and all who heard him were astounded at his intelligence and replies (Lk 2: 46).

The only phrase in this passage which seems to attract attention is that about Jesus' remarkable intelligence. The result then is that the picture many people have is of the young Jesus, not learning from the doctors (and, so, not really 'listening' to them), but questioning them as an examiner might. While Luke in this passage is anticipating the wisdom Jesus was to show during his ministry, he is also portraying him as, in Raymond E. Brown's words, 'intelligently curious about things religious' and is thus anticipating also the interest which Jesus was to show in debates over the law (*The Birth of the Messiah* , p 488).

There is, further, the gospel passage in which Jesus is spoken of as actually *growing in wisdom*:

> And Jesus increased in wisdom, in stature, and in favour with God and people (Lk 2: 52).

And there is the passage in which he is presented as even *admitting a lack of knowledge*. Mark and Matthew, for example, who, as I have pointed out above, present Jesus as giving in advance a remarkably detailed account of his passion and death, and who also portray him as talking in a detailed way of the future of the Jerusalem temple and of the coming days of tribulation (Mk 13: 5-27; Mt: 24: 4ff), still present him as openly admitting ignorance regarding 'when these things will happen':

> ... as for that day or hour, nobody knows it, neither the angels in heaven, nor the Son; no one but the Father (Mk 13: 32, *cf* Mt 24: 36).

There are, then, two sides to the story of the knowledge of Jesus as reflected in the gospels.

The third point is to recall what has been said in Chapter Two and Chapter Three about the origin, the nature, and the purpose of the gospels. The way in which the different gospels attribute, sometimes limited, and sometimes extraordinary knowledge to Jesus, reminds us, not just of the complexity of the man Jesus, but also of the complexity of the gospels themselves. It brings home to us, in a rather striking way, the fact that, in compiling their gospels, quite obviously the evangelists were not at all concerned about writing a straightforward *Life of Jesus*, careful to show how what is said in one passage is quite consistent with what has been said in another. Clearly they were intent, rather, on communicating to their respective audiences the Good News about Jesus, and on sharing with them who it was they now understood Jesus to be and what role he had in God's plan. Once we understand the origin and nature of the gospels, we cannot be all that surprised that we find the gospels sometimes presenting Jesus as speaking during his life as the eternal Son and Lord they *now* understood him to be. Indeed, because the gospels were written from the resurrection-perspective of faith in Jesus as *Messiah, Saviour, Son, Lord*, it is reasonable to argue that the texts which attribute limited knowledge to him are very likely indeed to represent Jesus as he lived in history.

* * *

Behind our thinking regarding the knowledge of Jesus there often lurks a docetism or a monophysitism of which we may not be at all conscious, and which may indicate that here we are going back on, and equivalently denying, what we profess in the creed about Jesus being 'true man' or 'truly human'. The hidden implications of the question of the knowledge of Jesus are expressed rather bluntly by Brian O. McDermott when he says:

Any view of the Christ-child at Christmas that invests the

child with an adult understanding of all that is going on around him ... is a form of monophysitism (*Word Become Flesh*, p 202).

When we say that Jesus was 'truly human', we need to realise that we must also say, to use the words of Luke,

And Jesus increased in wisdom ... (2: 52).

CHAPTER SIX

'Did he know he was God?'

Another way in which Christians might put the question 'Did he know he was God?' is: 'Was Jesus aware of his identity?' At the present stage in our reflections this is a better way of putting it since we have not yet discussed the sense in which Jesus might legitimately be said to be divine.

At the beginning of the previous chapter, I have argued that Christians have no choice but to answer to this question in some positive way. To say that God was present in Jesus in a unique way, but that Jesus was not in any way conscious of this, would be an impossible position to adopt: if what Christians call 'the Incarnation' did not affect Jesus in a conscious way it would not have been a human event at all. An obvious and difficult question then arises: how can we reconcile Jesus' awareness of his identity with what I have said about his being limited in knowledge? How, in other words, can we think of this awareness which Jesus must have had of his identity? The theologian whom I have found most helpful in this matter is Karl Rahner.

Reflections on human awareness
Rahner reflects on human awareness, or human consciousness, or human knowledge, in general terms. Usually, whenever we think about what it means to be aware of something, we seem to think immediately of the way in which we are aware of *an object*. The image which seems to suggest itself to us is that of the mind standing in front of an object, seeing it as a camera might see it, and being aware of it as an object before it. Rahner reminds us that it would be a mistake to think that every act of awareness is of this kind. There are, he points out, other ways of being aware of some-

thing. He draws our attention in particular to one most elementary state of awareness of which we all have experience but which is not at all of this kind. It is that most elementary direct awareness which we have of *ourselves* and which, indeed, we have had of ourselves throughout our whole conscious lives. Perhaps the best way of focusing our attention on it is to think of a very young child, an infant.

From the beginning of its conscious life, the infant is directly present to itself, is 'with itself', is aware of itself. This self-awareness is basic to everything which the infant does. It is, for example, because the infant is aware of *itself* that it cries for food. It is because it is first aware of *itself* that it reacts as it does to pain and responds as it does to affection and love. It takes very little reflection to see that if the infant were not first aware of itself, it would do none of those things. In all of these activities the infant acts and reacts because of what it experiences itself to be – that is, as *we* know, though the infant does not yet know it, a human being. This self-awareness also colours the infant's awareness of everything else: its consciousness of the presence of mother is related to, and coloured by, its awareness of itself – it experiences the presence of mother in terms, for example, of the security which it so needs and the warmth which it so enjoys. The infant's most fundamental and basic state of awareness, and that which makes possible and colours all other awareness, is, then, its direct presence to itself. What is true of the infant is, of course, equally true of ourselves.

Our basic awareness of ourselves

It is interesting to reflect on this self-awareness. Even though it is basic and all-pervasive in its influence on our lives, it is not at all, Rahner reminds us, the type of awareness suggested by the camera image. For in this instance there is no question at all of our seeing ourselves as an object. The infant, for example, who cries for food and reacts as it does to pain and human warmth precisely because it is aware of itself, does not at all 'stand before itself' as a camera looking at and 'seeing' an object. The infant never saw itself in that way and, so, is not at all aware of itself in that way. Its basic state of self-awareness – and ours – is, rather, a state of simply *experiencing* itself, a state of simply *consciously being* itself.

A most interesting, even paradoxical, truth emerges from this. It is that our most basic and fundamental state of awareness and consciousness, indeed, of knowledge, does not provide us with any information whatsoever! The infant, once again, though it is directly present to itself as the human being which it is, and, so, is conscious of itself in the most intimate way possible, still on the day of its birth knows absolutely nothing about itself in terms of factual knowledge. Indeed the infant spends the rest of its life learning facts about itself. Paradoxically, as Rahner observes, we all spend the rest of our lives learning about that human being whom we already always intimately experience ourselves to be. In that sense it can be said that we all spend our whole lives learning about what we had, in a most profound sense, already always 'known'.

Understanding our experience of ourselves
What happens in this second way of knowing is something on which we might reflect briefly. What happens is that, as we mature, we begin to stand back from ourselves, to reflect on ourselves, to learn facts about ourselves and, so, to understand ourselves in a new way – to know, for example, that we are 'a being', that we are 'a being who thinks and reflects', that we are 'a being who can love and be loved', that we are 'a being who has spiritual as well as bodily needs', and so forth. But, in so far as this new understanding of ourselves is a new understanding of the unique human being we are, it is a new understanding of who and what we already always experienced ourselves to be and, therefore, of what, in that sense, we already always 'knew'. We already

'knew' it in terms of *experience*, but not in terms of *concepts* or *understood facts*: we had not yet reflected on it or articulated it.

The self-awareness of Jesus

This sort of reflection, Rahner suggests, can help us to understand Jesus. In particular it can help us to understand three points about him.

Firstly it makes it possible for us to think of Jesus as having been aware, from his first conscious moment, of his identity as God's unique Son without having to think of him as always having known about this in the usual sense of that word. For we can think of Jesus' self-awareness in terms of that basic and direct awareness which each of us has of the unique human being who we are, in other words, of our own identity. If we do think of it in this way, then we do not have to think of Jesus as always having seen himself as a camera sees an 'object' and, so, as always having known who he was in the sense of always having reflected on himself and of always having understood who he was. We do not have to think of it in this way any more than we have to think of ourselves as always having understood who we are – even though, from the first moment of consciousness, we have been aware of ourselves as *this unique human being*.

Secondly, this broader understanding of awareness makes it possible for us to see how Jesus could, throughout his whole life, have been reflecting on his experience of himself, could have been growing in his understanding of this, and could always have been increasing in his ability to express anew, even for himself, his identity and his role. It would make it possible for us to see how, for example, Luke could say of Jesus what, we would all hope, could be said of ourselves:

> And Jesus increased in wisdom ... before God and people (2: 52).

It would even be possible for us to understand why Jesus might well indeed have been found during his life, particularly during his early years,

> ... sitting among the doctors, listening to them, and asking them questions ... (Lk 2: 46).

It would be possible for us to understand this regardless altogether of whether or not Luke's story refers to an actual historical event.

Thirdly, and most importantly, it makes it possible for us to see, or at least to have some insight into, how Jesus' relationship with the One whom in the agony scene at least he called *Abba*, in other words, his 'divine Sonship', had to be the most profound experience in his life, and how it must have permeated and coloured his whole experience of life and all his knowing. For if we think of his awareness of his relationship with God in terms of that basic state of awareness of self, we are then thinking of it in terms of that out of which all human experiences flow and which colours all other experiences. We are thinking of it, in that case, as the most fundamental experience of Jesus' life, that which was all-pervasive in its influence and which, therefore, affected everything which he perceived and said and did.

Jesus' presence to God

It is one thing, of course, to try to explain how Jesus, in always being present to himself, was always, in the sense explained, also aware of his own identity. But, we might well ask, in what sense could this presence to himself be a presence to *God*, and in what sense could this self-awareness have also been an awareness of God? Can we have any insight at all into how Jesus might have been present to and aware of God?

Once again the first point we need to remember in this context is that since, in the Christian view, Jesus was Son of God in a unique sense, in the last analysis his sense of God lies outside the range of our own personal experience. If this were not the case, then, obviously, we would have nothing at all to learn from Jesus about God.

This, however, does not mean that Jesus' presence to God and his sense of God is altogether and *in every respect* outside our experience. Here again we need to keep in mind the point which is being emphasised throughout this book, that is, that, unique though Jesus was, he was nonetheless a human being. His awareness of God, however unparalleled, was nonetheless a *creaturely* one – it was that of one who was still on his earthly journey towards full or 'heavenly' union with the Creator. Jesus, it ought to be remembered, is not the only one who, in the Christian view, was always present to God and aware of God. In the Christian view, we all are, and, in fact, always have been from the first moment of consciousness. Some reflection on our own creaturely presence to, and awareness of, God will, then, offer some insight into how, in broad terms at least, we might think of Jesus as being present to and aware of God.

The basic human awareness of God
Perhaps the easiest way of approaching this is to reflect briefly on a statement of St Augustine which everyone knows and to which, I think, most Christian believers will subscribe:

> You have made us for yourself, O Lord, and our hearts will not rest until they rest in you.

It is interesting to reflect carefully on the implications of this for the topic in question. The statement is explicitly saying that God, in creating us, has put within us a restlessness for the divine Self. It is quite obviously saying too that when we experience our deepest selves, 'our hearts', we experience this restlessness – otherwise we would not be aware of it. But, in saying this, it is necessarily also saying that in experiencing our deepest selves, we are also, in some way or other, actually experiencing God. For, if we did not experience God in *some* way, we could not experience a restlessness for God: how could we possibly be restless for 'someone' of whom we did not have any hint at all and, so, did not experience in any way at all? So, when, as believers, we say with St Augustine that our hearts are, and always have been, restless for God, we are saying, whether we are aware of this or not, that, in being present to and aware of our deepest selves, we are, and always have been, actually present to God – in some way at least. We are, in fact, echoing Edward Schillebeeckx's words:

To stand before oneself is to stand before God.

In the present context two points need to be made about this basic human awareness of God.

The first is that in saying that self-awareness is also awareness of God, we obviously do not intend to say that our self-awareness gives us that 'view' or 'vision' of God which, we believe, the blessed in heaven have and which would enable us to participate in God's own knowledge – a 'view' or 'vision' of God which would, of course, be altogether incompatible with our earthly state. Here we might recall what Paul says:

Now we are seeing a dim reflection in a mirror; but then we shall be seeing face to face (1 Cor 13: 12).

The second point is that when we say that in being present to ourselves we 'stand before God', we are not saying that we necessarily have any mental picture or image of God. The infant who is restless for food has no mental picture or image at all of what 'food' is. But, having some experience of something which might satisfy its hunger, it has, in that sense, some experience, however vague and unconceptualized, of what we call 'food'.

In experiencing our deepest selves, we are experiencing God, then, not at all, as it were, formally, that is, as that 'divine Being' of our imaginings. Rather, we are experiencing

God in a much more anonymous and vague way: we are experiencing God in terms, for example, of that unimaginable *Rest* for which we are endlessly restless, or as that unimaginable *Fulfilment* towards which our whole being is oriented and for which, as Augustine says, we are made. In a word, we are experiencing God only, but nonetheless profoundly, in the sense that, permeating all our experiences, there are, as E. H. Ebner puts it, vague, though very powerful, 'hints and intimations' of

> ... what beckons us dimly yet ever remains out of reach.

We are experiencing God in the sense that

> ... in all our thought and language there is a resonance of the Infinite, as its deepest background ... (*A New Catechism*, p 17).

Jesus' awareness of God

These reflections on our own creaturely and human experience of God should at least open up for us a way of thinking about the basic awareness of God which Jesus had. They should, for example, show how it is not at all necessary to think of this in terms of that ecstatic awareness of God which we associate with the happy, blissful, heavenly state of those who have arrived at the goal of their life's journey. They should show us too that we do not at all have to think of Jesus' presence to God in terms of a 'formal', face-to-face presence to the 'divine Being' of our human imaginings. The reflections make it possible for us to think of Jesus as being aware of God in a much more 'anonymous' way. We can think of him as being aware of God in terms, for example, of that dark *Source* of his being in which he experienced himself as being ultimately grounded. We can think of him as being aware of God, somewhat as we all are, in terms of that mysterious *Unlimit* towards which he experienced himself to be oriented and powerfully drawn. Or we can think of him as experiencing God in terms of that limitless *Horizon* which, in Karl Rahner's words,

... always encircles and upholds the small area of our everyday experience of knowing and acting, our knowledge of reality and our free action (*Theological Investigations*, vol 9, p 122).

In general terms, and in this matter we can only speak in general terms, we might, then, think of Jesus as one who was given the gift of an unfathomably deep sense of, and attunement to, and intimacy with, that nameless and unimaginable *Mystery*, that vague limitless *Horizon*, of which we have all some experience.

* * *

The gospels give us access to the truth about Jesus as understood in the light of resurrection-faith. Taken just at their face-value, they could give us a wrong impression of Jesus as he made his pilgrim journey through life towards the Father. The Letters, which also are a very large, and a very important part of the Christian scriptures, are not the unusual documents which gospels are. Being letters, they are of a more familiar and straightforward type. In regard to the Jesus of history, Jesus the pilgrim, they sometimes give us a very startling picture of how life really was for Jesus. We get a glimpse of this in the following passage from the Letter to the Hebrews, a passage which can hardly leave us in any doubt but that Jesus was indeed, to use the phrase I have used so often, 'a humble human being':

For it is not as if we had a high priest who was incapable of feeling our weaknesses with us; but we have one who has been tempted in every way that we are, though he is without sin ... During his life on earth, he offered up prayer and entreaty, aloud and in silent tears, to the one who had the power to save him out of death, and he submitted so humbly that his prayer was heard. Although he was Son, he learnt to obey through suffering ... (4:15-16, 5: 7-9).

The uniqueness of Jesus

CHAPTER SEVEN

'Born of the Virgin Mary'

A useful way of introducing the Christian view of the uniqueness of Jesus is, I believe, to talk about the virginal conception of Jesus. This, after all, is the way in which both Luke and Matthew introduce it in their respective present-ations of the Good News of Jesus – these, it will be recalled, are the two gospels which have infancy narratives.

Virginal conception

We need to understand what it is to which the term 'virgin-al conception' refers. I find that, today particularly, it needs to be emphasised that the virginal conception of Jesus is to be clearly distinguished from the Roman Catholic doctrine of the Immaculate Conception of Mary. The latter has to do with Mary's own conception in her own mother's womb. It has nothing at all to do with her origins or with paternity, but speaks only of a spiritual event. Here we do not have to explain in any precise way what the doctrine of the Immac-ulate Conception of Mary means. It is enough to say, in passing, that, in very general terms, it expresses the convict-ion that from the very beginning of her existence – from her conception – Mary was, in the words of Luke, 'highly favoured' (1:29) and was specially prepared spiritually by God for her role as mother of Jesus. The virginal conception of Jesus, on the other hand, talks about Jesus' conception in Mary's womb. It describes Jesus as being conceived in the womb of a woman who was still a virgin and, therefore, as being one who had no human father.

What, we might ask, is this virginal conception all about?

Two common misconceptions

It is necessary at the outset to say what the virginal conception of Jesus is *not* about. This is necessary because of two misconceptions which are common today.

First, it would be very wrong to think that the virginal conception of Jesus was necessary so as to make it possible for *God* to be the Father of Jesus, on the grounds that human fatherhood would *automatically* exclude the divine Fatherhood. To think in this way would be to put the Fatherhood of God on the same level as human fatherhood. It would, then, be to think that the Christian community sees God as the physical father of Jesus. But that would be to misunderstand its position grossly. The precise sense in which the Christian community does understand Jesus to be the Son of God will be discussed more formally and more explicitly in the following chapters. This much, however, must be said here: the Christian community does not see God as taking the place of the human father in Jesus' case in such as way as to be 'himself' the physical, biological father of Jesus. In the Christian view, Jesus is not one who was conceived of a human mother and a divine father in the way that pagan demi-gods were imagined to have been. Jesus is not seen as a 'mixture' of the divine and the human; he is not, as the theologian (later Cardinal) Joseph Ratzinger reminds us, 'half God, half man'. Jesus is no less than one hundred per cent a human being.

Since God is not believed to be the biological father of Jesus, since the divine Sonship of which Christians speak is of a different kind from this, this divine Sonship would not be automatically excluded had Jesus had a human father. As Joseph Ratzinger said when writing on this subject in 1968:

> According to the faith of the Church, the Sonship of Jesus does not rest on the fact that Jesus had no human father; the doctrine of Jesus' divinity would not be affected if Jesus had been the product of a normal human marriage.

For the Sonship of which faith speaks is not a biological
but an ontological fact, an event not in time but in God's
eternity ... (*Introduction to Christianity*, p 298).

Thus we find that in the scriptures, for example, the divine
Sonship of Jesus is not seen as dependent on the virginal
conception. The virginal conception is mentioned only by
Matthew and Luke, and by these only in their infancy narratives. But even if there had been no infancy narratives and,
so, no mention in scripture of the virginal conception, we
would still know, even from scripture, about Jesus' divine
Sonship. We would know it, for example, from the accounts
of the baptism and transfiguration of Jesus, and from the
theologies of John and Paul, neither of whom make any reference whatsoever to the virginal conception of Jesus.

It would be very wrong, secondly, to see the virginal conception as being a negative comment on the sexual union of
man and wife. Rarely, of course, do we find anyone actually
saying that it is. But that it is such is very often implied in the
way people think and talk Mary's virginity. It is implied, for
example, when it is assumed that to have entered into marital sex with her husband, Joseph, would necessarily have
been an obstacle to Mary's perfection and, so, would necessarily have left her less holy. Marital sex, it may not be forgotten, is created and willed and blessed by God. To think
that it is in any way ugly or tainted or undignified and that,
therefore, it would have been unbecoming for Jesus to have
been conceived in the way in which we all were, would be-
tray a very serious failure to understand the true dignity of
sexual married love. Here a point to which Raymond E.
Brown draws attention is worth noting. It is that in the
infancy stories in the gospels Mary herself is presented as
having actually chosen the married state; the virginal conception comes as God's idea, not as her choice initially.

This is not at all to overlook the great religious value of
what is often referred to as 'the life of consecrated virginity'.
The voluntary renunciation of marriage can indeed be a

striking and radical witness to a particular person's religious belief. It can be this by pointing in an unusual and very
striking way to the person's conviction that the values of
this world, even the noblest and most beautiful of these, are
not, after all, the only ones. But, it needs to be remembered,
the renunciation of marriage will be a striking and radical
statement of this religious belief only if marriage is freely
renounced precisely because it is seen to be so basic and so
beautiful and so good. To renounce something which is
seen to be tainted or ugly is something which can be seen to
make sense even in terms of an enclosed world-system. The
voluntary renunciation of marriage precisely because it is
seen to be so good would make no sense at all in terms of
such an enclosed system. It makes sense only in terms of belief in values other than even the most noble ones of this
world.

The appropriateness of the virginal conception of Jesus is
not, then, to be found in any inappropriateness whatsoever
in the sexual union of man and wife. To think that it does
would be to miss altogether the significance of this event.
As Joseph Ratzinger puts it:

> The virgin birth is not a lesson in asceticism (as above, p
> 210).

(A point worth noting here is that we find theologians often
speaking of the 'the virgin birth' when they really mean the
virginal *conception*).

The biblical background

Our best clue to the true significance of the virginal concept–
ion of Jesus is to be found, as we might indeed expect, in the
Bible itself. It is not that there is any other instance in the
Bible of a virginal conception – the manner of Jesus' conception is, of course, unique in the Bible. There are, however, in
the Bible several instances of unusual births. The unexpected
birth of a son to Abraham and Sarah is well known (Gen 17).
So too is the unexpected birth of John the Baptist to Zech-

ariah and Elizabeth (Lk 1: 5f). Not so well known, perhaps, but, as Joseph Ratzinger in particular points out, equally important in this context, are the stories of the unexpected births of Samson (Jdgs 13) and of Samuel (1 Sam 1f). Some reflection on the stories of these unusual births will help us to understand the significance of the virginal conception of Jesus.

Three points in particular about these births need to be noted.

Firstly in all these cases the parents in question are described as having no hope, humanly speaking, of conceiving a child. Abraham and Sarah are old and well past child-bearing age (Gen 17). The wife of Manoah (I refer to her as in the story), who was to be the mother of Samson, was, as the angel in the story reminded her, 'barren' (Jdgs 13). Of Hannah also, who was to be the mother of Samuel, the Bible says 'Yahweh had made her barren' (1 Sam 1: 6) – the Bible is, of course, here reflecting the very primitive ideas of the day. Elizabeth and Zechariah, Luke says, were old and their marriage was childless:

> ... they were childless: Elizabeth was barren and they were both getting on in years (1: 7).

Secondly, we will note that in each case God is represented as intervening and blessing the couple with a child. Accordingly, the child is afterwards seen to be the result of God's graciousness and blessing. It is thanks to *God* that these 'barren' marriages became fruitful. Sarah, on the birth of her son, says:

> God has given me cause to laugh; all those who hear of it will laugh with me (Gen 21: 6).

Hannah says of her own child:

> This is the child I prayed for, and Yahweh granted me what I asked him (1 Sam 27).

When Elizabeth conceived, she said:

The Lord had done this for me ... now that it has pleased him to take away the humiliation I suffered among people (Lk 1: 25).

Mary is told about Elizabeth:

... she whom people called barren is now in her sixth month, for nothing is impossible to God (Lk 1: 36-38).

What was humanly impossible, God was seen to have made possible.

The third point is that in each of these cases the child who is born turns out to exercise a key-function in God's dealings with Israel. Isaac, the son of Abraham and Sarah, marked the beginning of a new race; Samson was the great saviour of Israel in its crucial struggle against the Philistines; Samuel was a key-figure in Israel's becoming a kingdom; it was John the Baptist who, in the gospels, heralded the beginning of the new era brought by Jesus. Each of these unexpected births marked, therefore, a new important initiative by God at a critical stage in Israel's history. In each case it was as a result of God's initiative that a saviour of some kind was given.

The point can easily be seen. It is that it is *God* who takes the initiative in Israel's history. Israel's salvation is not, in the last analysis, the result of human achievement, but of God's graciousness. It is as impossible for the race itself to bring about salvation as it was for these 'barren' couples to have these children. In the last analysis, the human race can only let the gift of salvation be bestowed on it.

The significance of the conception of Jesus
It is against this background, and in this light, that the significance of the virginal conception of Jesus is to be understood. The point being made in the case of the conception of Jesus is basically the same as that made in these other cases. Jesus, the Saviour, is not the result of human achievement. He is a human being in whom God has taken an initiative in human affairs. He is a human being in whom God has taken

a surprise initiative in human affairs. For if it was a divine gift for those 'barren' couples, who were yearning for a child, to have their child, it was a totally unexpected divine gift for a virgin, Mary, to give birth to Jesus. As far as producing Jesus is concerned, the race itself, and not just Mary, can only say:

> But how can this come about, since I am a virgin? (Lk 1: 34).

For the coming of Jesus, the race too must await the words:

> The Holy Spirit will come upon you ... and the power of the Most High will cover you with its shadow (Lk 1: 35).

As far as giving birth to Jesus is concerned, the race must say

> Let it be done to me ... (Lk 1: 37).

Jesus marks the beginning of a *new creation* by God. Just as 'in the beginning' God's spirit hovered over the water, the womb of all life, and brought forth new life, now the same Spirit came upon Mary and brought forth the Christ. Jesus is, then, the New Adam (Rom 5: 12-21). As the biblical scholar, Bruce Vawter, says:

> Jesus is the son of no earthly father but only of God because with him begins a whole new creation of man, a new human race. This new Adam appears as son of God and without other father precisely as the first Adam appeared (Lk 3: 38) ... (*This Man Jesus*, p 191).

The point of the virginal conception of Jesus is well summarised by Karl Rahner. Jesus was conceived virginally,

> ... not as if the world were evil or marriage not an institution of his own founding, nor as if the sexual union between man and wife were not of God's own founding, nor as if the normal, natural coming into existence of a human being were in some way tainted with a dubious slur ...

He was conceived virginally rather because

> the earthly fabric of things, even of the noblest weave, is here interrupted (*Mother of the Lord*, p. 68).

The emphasis

Here it is interesting, especially because of certain ideas which seem current today, to reflect again on the gospel stories regarding the conception of Jesus and on the emphasis in these. In particular we need to look at the place which virginity has in the accounts. A Latin American bishop, Paulo Eduardo Andrade Ponte writes that if one were to judge by the sermons one hears and the spiritual books one reads, one would think that the whole emphasis in this context was on Mary's virginity and that it was for the sake of preserving her virginity that the conception of Jesus was 'supernatural'. If we examine the gospel narratives, however, we will find that the emphasis there is not at all on Mary's virginity. It is, rather, on *the unique involvement of God in Jesus' conception*. So, as the bishop points out, it is not at all in order to preserve Mary's virginity that Jesus is described as being conceived of the Holy Spirit, but, rather, the opposite: it is for the purpose of emphasising Jesus' uniqueness that the virginity is important. Joseph A. Fitzmyer says of the accounts in Matthew and Luke of the virginal conception of Jesus:

> ... their main thrust is an affirmation about Jesus, not about Mary ever-Virgin (*A Christological Catechism*, p 34).

* * *

The message of the virginal conception gets to the heart of the Christian conviction regarding the uniqueness of Jesus. Though Jesus is a human being, he is not, in the Christian view, just one other human being. Christians who believe this man to be unique believe him to be unique, not basically because of what he said or did, important though all this is;

they believe him to be unique basically because they believe
him to be one in whom *God* is involved and present, in a
unique way, from the very first moment of his conception.

Very simply, it is to this Christian conviction that expressions like 'the divine Sonship of Jesus' and 'the divinity of
Jesus' refer. These expressions, it is important to know, are
nothing other than attempts to articulate this conviction.
Understanding what Christian belief means by these terms
is, then, a matter of understanding *how*, in the Christian
view, God is present and involved in this human life. In
other words, it is a matter of understanding what, in the
Christian view, is the relationship between this human being, Jesus of Nazareth, and God.

It is this aspect of the Christian understanding of Jesus
which will be examined in the following chapters.

CHAPTER EIGHT

'Jesus is God'

I

'Jesus is God'. This statement is taken by many people to be a simple and accurate summary of the Christian understanding of the relation between Jesus and God. So much so, indeed, that it is commonly used as a touchstone of orthodoxy in this matter: to accept the statement unquestioningly seems to be enough to prove one's orthodoxy in regard to Christ; to say anything which seems to be at all at variance with it is enough to leave one's orthodoxy regarding the central truth of christianity at best suspect.

The statement 'Jesus is God' has, of course, a long history in Christian piety. However this statement is not at all the simple and accurate summary of Christian belief about Jesus and God that it is commonly taken to be. It is not, therefore, as good a touchstone of orthodoxy in this matter as it is often assumed to be.

Two statements

The limitations of this summary-statement can perhaps best be seen by comparing it with another similar-type statement typical of ones we make everyday. To demonstrate this we shall, then, compare two statements:

Statement 1: *John is the fourth evangelist*
Statement 2: *Jesus is God*

It is easily seen that these two statements are similar in form. In each case there is a subject-term and a predicate-term, and these are joined by the word 'is'. In each case this word 'is' affirms a relationship between the subject and the predicate terms. Since the same word, 'is', describes the re-

lationship in both statements, it would appear that the very
same relationship is being affirmed in both cases. It would
appear, then, that it is stated that the relationship between
Jesus of Nazareth and God is exactly the same as that between John and the fourth evangelist. In other words, it
would appear that the man Jesus of Nazareth is here said to
be God in the same sense that John is said to be the fourth
evangelist. It takes only a little reflection, however, to see
that this cannot be the case – cannot, that is, if the statement
about Jesus and God makes any sense at all and is an orthodox statement. This can be seen by taking the statements in
turn.

Statement 1: *John is the fourth evangelist:*
Here it is said that the man 'John' is the fourth evangelist in
the sense that he is simply identical with the fourth evangelist. (It is not, of course, implied that the notion 'John' is identical with the notion 'fourth evangelist'.) The subject and the
predicate-term are so identified here that it is implied that
wherever John is or was, the fourth evangelist necessarily is
or was. These are so identified that it is possible for us to reverse the terms and say: The fourth evangelist is John. The
word 'is' in this sentence means is *simply identical with*.

Statement 2: *Jesus is God*:
It does not have this meaning in the statement about Jesus
and God – it cannot if this statement is true. The subject-
term here, Jesus, obviously refers to a man from Nazareth,
and so, refers to one who is creaturely. It refers, therefore, to
one who is limited, who was born in time, and who died.
The predicate-term, God, refers to the Creator. It refers,
therefore, to 'One' who is not a creature, who is unlimited,
eternal and immortal. One who is creaturely, limited, temp-
oral, and mortal, cannot be simply *identical* with the God
who, as Creator, created him, and who is unlimited, eternal
and immortal. Whatever unity between subject and predicate terms is intended to be affirmed here, it cannot, if the

statement is to make sense at all, be one of simple identification of subject and predicate terms. So, while the first statement so identifies the terms that it allows us to reverse
them, the second statement, if it is true to Christian belief,
cannot be doing this. Christians, who say, for example, that
it was God who took the initiative in the coming-to-be of
Jesus, cannot, and should not, say 'God is Jesus'. Nor can
they say, if they are true to their Christian belief, that wherever, and only wherever, the man from Nazareth was, God
is. The man from Nazareth is not believed to have been, for
example, in Egypt at the time of the Exodus. God, however,
is believed to have been involved in this event.

'is' with a difference

Jesus, then, is not God is the same sense as John is the fourth
evangelist. This means that if the statement 'Jesus is God' is
true, clearly the word 'is' has a different meaning here from
that which it has in the statement about the fourth evangelist. And since the latter is typical of statements which we
make everyday, even many times at day, it follows that, as
Karl Rahner often emphasises, the word 'is' in the Jesus-
statement has a different meaning from that which it normally has in everyday similar-type statements. So we find
Joseph Ratzinger, for example, when speaking, not exactly
of Jesus being God, but of the converse of this, of God being
man, expresses his thought thus:

> … God as Son in the man Jesus draws the creature man to
> himself, so that he himself 'is' man (*Introduction to Christ-*
> *ianity*, p 208; *cf* the German original).

A most important point emerges here. It is that in the sentence 'Jesus is God', if this is a true statement of Christian
belief, that small word 'is', which we use so often and so
simply everyday, has actually been given some new meaning, yet for the most part no warning or hint whatsoever of
this most important fact is given. (We will notice, however,
that Joseph Ratzinger, by the way he writes 'is' in the above
sentence does give that warning.)

It is because of this that the statement 'Jesus is God' is not at all the simple and accurate summary-statement of Christian belief which it is so often assumed to be. For if it is taken to be the simple everyday-type 'is'-statement that it appears to be, then it is not accurate. And if it is accurate, then it is by no means the simple statement which it appears to be. The statement 'Jesus is God' cannot, then, be accepted as a simple touchstone of orthodoxy with regard to Jesus. One could very well reject this statement and yet be profoundly orthodox – in fact if the statement is intended to mean what, on the face of it, it seems to mean, one has to reject it if one wants to be orthodox. On the other hand one could accept it and not be orthodox at all – for if one takes it at its face-value one is then saying something which does not make sense at all, which cannot be true, and which cannot, therefore, be a Church dogma.

A complex relationship

These reflections on the limitations of the statement 'Jesus is God' force us to look again, in a preliminary way here, at the official Christian position regarding the relationship between Jesus and God. When we do look at this we find that, in its official teaching, the Christian community does not in fact understand this relationship to be one of simple identity as the statement 'Jesus is God' would suggest. In fact, it sees it as being a very complex relationship – a much more complex one, indeed, than people sometimes think.

Here it is useful to recall something of the history of the Christian community's struggle to express the nature of the exact relationship between Jesus and God. During the first centuries of its life, it will be remembered, the Church was deeply divided on several occasions by controversies as to how the relationship is to be understood and expressed. One after another, we will recall, scholarly people like Arius (c 315), Apollinarius (c 360), Nestorius (c 431), Eutyches (c 444), and Sergius I (c 633) struggled to understand the precise nature of the relationship and each put forward his own theory about it. Each of the theories of these men, however, was rejected as false because it failed to do justice to the true Christian conviction regarding Jesus. An indication of how complex the matter was found to be during these years is the rather ironical situation which arose: scholarly people who set out staunchly to defend orthodoxy against one extreme position were sometimes found to have themselves gone to the opposite extreme and, so, to have also ended up distorting the truth. The controversies of these centuries culminated in the Council of Chalcedon which, in 451, summarised what had been learned from these years of reflection and discussion and produced its well known statement of Christian belief regarding the person of Jesus. To understand the true Christian position we need, then, to know what this summary-statement says.

At this stage in our study two points in particular about Chalcedon's statement need to be noted.

The first – and it is a very important one – has to do with the complexity of the statement. It is far from being a simple three-word statement like 'Jesus is God'. It is, in fact, so nuanced a statement that, in the English translation, it runs to over 300 words!

The second is that, broadly speaking, Chalcedon's Decree emphasises two truths about the relationship between Jesus and God; the first is that there is a unique *unity* between Jesus and God and the second is that there is a *distinction* between them.

Unity

That Christian faith has always understood Jesus and God to be united in a unique way is, of course, something which is attested throughout the Christian scriptures themselves. Thus the prologue to John introduces Jesus as being united to the 'Word' who 'was God':

In the beginning was the Word:
the Word was with God
and the Word was God.
...
The Word was made flesh,
he lived among us ... (1:1ff).

This unique unity is attested also in the scriptures' many references to Jesus being 'the Son of God' – for example in sermons in the Acts of the Apostles, and in the stories of Jesus' baptism and transfiguration. It is attested too in the way in which Jesus is presented, especially in the discourses in John, as speaking about the very intimate unity which there is between himself, the 'Son', and 'the Father'.

The unique unity which Christians believe exists between Jesus and God is something which has also always been upheld by the Christian community's *official teaching*. It was upheld in a particularly striking way when the Council of Ephesus (431) taught, in the context of the views of Nestorius, that Mary, being the mother of Jesus, was, by that very fact, also the mother of God's 'Word' in our midst, and was, in that sense (we shall examine it more closely in the following chapters), 'the mother of God' (*theotokos*). It is not surprising, then, to find that the Decree of Chalcedon also, in summarising Christian belief about Jesus, emphasises this unique unity between Jesus and God or, more precisely, between Jesus and the 'Word of God', or, to use the Greek term for the 'Word', the *Logos*.

The reader will, no doubt, have noticed that, all the time, I am speaking here of this unity only in very vague terms. I am doing this on purpose because the precise nature of the unity in question is not something which I wish to discuss at this stage.

One point, however, needs to be made immediately about this unity – and it needs to be made as strongly as possible. It is that the unity between Jesus and the 'Word' of God has always been understood by the Christian community to be, in the strict sense of this word, *unique* – in other words to be a unity which is different from any other in our experience. So, referring to the word 'is' which is so often used to express this unity, Karl Rahner says,

> The meaning of the copula 'is' rests here on a unique union (such as is not found elsewhere and remains profoundly mysterious) ... (*Sacramentum Mundi*, vol 3, p 196).

So different is the unity thought to be, it needs to be emphasised, that theology uses – indeed has had to coin – a special term to describe it. That term, as those familiar with the language of theology will recall, is the term 'hypostatic', a term which comes from the Greek word *hypostasis* used in this context by, for example, the Council of Chalcedon. This point about the unity between Jesus and the 'Word' of God being, according to Christian teaching, simply unique is one which tends to be forgotten. When it is forgotten, and when the impression is given that the unity in question is simply of an everyday kind, then an essential part of the Christian belief about Jesus is forgotten and an altogether wrong and misleading impression is given.

Distinction

Unity is not the whole story of the relationship between Jesus and God or, rather, the 'Word' of God. In the true Christian view there is also *distinction* between them – a point which is also often forgotten but which, again, may not be forgotten if we are to have a correct understanding of Jesus.

The very fact that Jesus, as he lived in history and as he is perceived in faith, was a real human being itself shows that there was some distinction between him and the 'Word' who is God: human beings, we know, simply are not the same as God; God, being Creator is, by definition, radically different from all created beings and, therefore, from human beings. Since a human being cannot be simply identical with God, or with the 'Word' who is God, whatever unity exists between the human being Jesus of Nazareth and the 'Word' of God must be such as allows also for distinction.

Scripture itself, of course, witnesses to a distinction between Jesus and God. It witnesses to it when, for example, it presents Jesus, though 'Son' and 'Word', as acting in a creaturely way before God – as when it presents him as praying to God, as adoring God, or as feeling abandoned by God. Unless the author of the Letter to the Hebrews, for example, saw a distinction between Jesus and God, he could hardly have said of Jesus what I have earlier quoted him as saying of him:

> During his life on earth, he offered up prayer and entreaty, aloud and in silent tears, to the one who had the power to save him out of death, and he submitted so humbly that his prayer was heard (5: 7).

Nor could Mark and Matthew have put into the mouth of Jesus the words of the psalm:

> My God, my God, why have you deserted me? (Mk 15: 34; Mt 27: 46).

For, we can hardly think that in passages like these the sacred authors were representing Jesus as talking to, and being heard by, One who was simply *identical* with himself! Here we must allow for the fact that in the Christian scriptures the word 'God' usually refers to 'the Father', and that Jesus himself is generally spoken of as the 'Word' or the 'Son'. But even allowing for that, the fact that Jesus is presented as praying to the 'Father' still shows that the scriptures do not see him as being simply *identical* even with the eternal 'Son' or 'Word': since the 'Word is God', and since there is only one God, there would still be question of God being presented as praying to, and being 'forsaken' by, the divine Self. Whatever interaction there might be between the 'Father' and the eternal 'Son' within God, it cannot be that the eternal 'Son', as existing simply within the Godhead, prays in petition to the 'Father', as Jesus is presented as doing, or that the eternal 'Son' eternally feels 'forsaken' by the 'Father'. So, however intimate and unique scripture understands Jesus' unity with the 'Word' of God to be, it sees this as embracing some real distinction between him and God. However scripture understood 'the divine Sonship' of Jesus, it did not see it as meaning that Jesus was simply identical with God considered even as eternal 'Son', being in no way whatsoever distinct from God.

As regards Church dogma, people, I find, seem to think of this in particular as insisting – firmly – on just *unity* between Jesus and God. This, however, is not at all the case. Here we need to recall the fifth-century monk, Eutyches, referred to in Chapter One, whose view was that the human reality in Jesus was absorbed into the divine and, so, lost its separateness and distinctness: Eutyches spoke, therefore, only of a real unity between Jesus and God. The Council of Chalcedon, however, rejected his view and insisted that, in Jesus, the human and divine realities ('natures') were united in such a way that each retained its own separate and distinct properties. The words of the Council are important and worth quoting:

> The difference of natures will never be abolished by their being united, but rather the properties of each remain unimpaired.

According to this definitive teaching of the Church, then, the human reality ('nature') in Jesus, in its unity with the divine, retains its own distinctness vis-à-vis the divine. This again is something which Christians who are familiar with the catechism will know: they will remember that, according to the teaching of the Church, the unity between Jesus and God is one in which, as it is often said, 'two natures' remained distinct.

'Nature'

Some comment on the word 'nature' is called for here, especially for the benefit of those who are familiar with the language of the catechism and of theology. To refer to the human
reality in Jesus as 'a human nature' is, in modern English at
least, to run the risk of misleading people. This is particularly
the case when, as often happens, a human 'nature' is
thought of as being distinct from a human 'person'. To talk
in this way today can easily give the impression that Jesus'
human reality, 'nature', was a characterless ('impersonal'),
inert 'block' of humanity (to use Paul Tillich's word) having
no independence or freedom or initiative of its own vis-à-
vis God. This, however, would be to give a very wrong impression. The original word used by the Council of Chalcedon (the Greek word *physis*), which the English word 'nature' is used to translate, cannot have had this connotation of
inertness and lack of freedom and spontaneity. It did not
imply, for example, that the human in Jesus lacked its own
'personality' in the everyday sense of that word. That this is
so is very clear. It is clear from the teaching of a later council, the Third Council of Constantinople (681). This council,
to which there was reference already in Chapter One, made
it clear, in the context of the views of the Patriarch Sergius I,
that Jesus had human freedom. It made it clear, then, that
the human reality or 'nature' (*physis*) in Jesus stood free and
independent before God. In making this clear, it showed
that what classical theology refers to as a human 'nature'
was far from being the impersonal, inert 'block' of humanity
which the word might suggest today. It shows that the word
'nature' (*physis*) refers, rather, as Karl Rahner especially, so
often and so convincingly points out, to a real and complete
human being, who, like every human being, stood before
God independent and free. It showed, then, that this human
reality which, was 'hypostatically' united to the 'Word' of
God was not at all like a 'block' of humanity, but was rather
a human being who, as such, remained also distinct from

God. (The use of the word 'person' in the context of Jesus will be commented on later, in Appendix III, in the context of 'hypostatic union'.)

A preliminary statement

At this point we are able to state, in a preliminary way, how the Christian position regarding the relationship between Jesus and God might legitimately be understood and how it is being understood here. Jesus of Nazareth is a free and independent human being and, as such, remains different and distinct from God. He is, however, a human being who is united to the 'Word' of God in a unique way – he is united to this 'Word', to use Karl Rahner's words again, in a union 'such as is not found elsewhere and remains profoundly mysterious'. Jesus is, in fact, the human being who is united to the 'Word' of God 'hypostatically', to use the technical, theological term.

In the light of the summary statement given here, it becomes clearer even than before why the simple statement 'Jesus is God' is a very unsatisfactory summary-statement of Christian belief. Taken as it is, the statement asserts only a unity between Jesus and God. It makes no reference whatsoever to the distinction which there is between them, and, so, it gives the impression that Jesus and God are simply identical. We can see, however, that, in doing this it does not do justice at all to Christian belief. Consequently, it makes it very difficult for us to understand Jesus and his true relationship with God.

In Chapter One I pointed out that it is impossible to understand the *divine* in Jesus without taking him seriously as a human being – for, in the Christian understanding, it is a human being who is the unique Son of God. It ought now to be clear that it is equally impossible to understand the *unity* which, according to Christian belief, exists between Jesus and God without taking into account the distinction which there is between them – for, again in the Christian view, this is a unity between a human being and the 'Word' who is God and, therefore, a unity of realities 'which' in their unity also retain their distinctness.

II

About putting it in a nutshell

How is it, the reader might wonder, that we tend to forget about this distinction between Jesus and God and to concentrate only on the unity between them? The answer, it seems to me, is to be found in our fondness for 'nutshell-statements'. Generally speaking, we like to put a complex matter simply – we like 'to put it in a nutshell'. Putting it in a nutshell, however, has its dangers. In order to be put in a nutshell a complex matter has to be very compressed, and when it is compressed its original complex shape and contours tend to be lost. We may know, of course, that our nutshell statement is an over-simplification. If pressed on the matter, we may very well be able to clarify and explain any difficulties which arise from our over-simplification. Nutshell statements, however, are so very neat and handy that we begin to use them frequently. As a result, they are liable to become very much part of us and of our thinking. When this happens, these statements can begin to influence our thinking in a very subtle and perhaps unnoticed way. They can even become principles guiding it.

In my experience, this has happened with the statement 'Jesus is God'. People may know, deep down at least, that the union between Jesus and God is understood by the Church to be unique 'such as is not found elsewhere and remains profoundly mysterious'. They may even know, especially if they are familiar with the language of theology, that theology had to coin the special term 'hypostatic' to describe it. They may, then, be able to explain that in this statement 'is' means 'is hypostatically united to', and that this is not at all what 'is' means in everyday statements: John, they might point out, is said to be simply identical with the fourth evangelist, and is not at all said to be 'hypostatically united to' the fourth evangelist. Deep down most Christians know well that the relationship between Jesus and God is a much more complex one that this simple statement 'Jesus is God' would suggest.

However, it is my experience that this nutshell statement 'Jesus is God' is so familiar and so widely used that it exerts a profound influence on the way very many people think about Jesus. Very often even those who know deep down that it is a compression of a very complex matter, seem, surprisingly, to have themselves become its captives. Despite themselves, they too seem, at one level of their thinking at least, to take the statement 'Jesus is God' as though it were a typical everyday-statement. Consequently, they simply identify Jesus with God. This simple identification is so common that I myself now know from experience that when, in the course of a talk, I am writing or mentioning the word 'Jesus', many people present are actually reading or hearing a different word, that is, the word 'God'. Furthermore very many people make this understanding of Jesus a touchstone against which they test the orthodoxy of what is said about him – especially, I find, if someone confronts them with the limitations of Jesus. So, for example, if someone says that Jesus was creaturely – something which is, of course, profoundly orthodox – he or she is likely to be challenged, in the name of orthodoxy, with the objection 'But Jesus is God'. What is meant by this in the context is that since Jesus is identical with God, he cannot be creaturely. There is, of course, a sad irony here. The person who uses this statement in this way to defend orthodoxy is actually interpreting it in an unorthodox way: he or she is taking the statement simply at its face value! In a sense, of course, this ought not to be too surprising. For once we begin to compress into three words – or, rather, into the single word 'is' – what the Council of Chalcedon, in the light of difficulties which had actually arisen at the time, took over 300 words to summarise, we can take it that we are short-circuiting the truth and, so, putting ourselves at serious risk of doing damage to it.

The use of the name 'Jesus'

A comment on the use of the name 'Jesus' might be helpful at this point. This name, as we know, is used by Christians to refer to the man from Nazareth and to the eternal 'Son' or 'Word' of God, and it is not always clear in what sense it is used of the 'Word'. (The word 'Christ', I ought to mention, though often taken to be Jesus's surname, is not in fact a person's name but refers rather to a role or function which Christians believe Jesus to have exercised in God's plan.) To whom precisely, we might ask, does the name 'Jesus' refer?

Throughout this book the name 'Jesus' is used to refer primarily and directly to the first century human being Jesus of Nazareth. Because of the unique relationship which, according to Christian belief, there is between this man and the eternal 'Word', it is seen as referring also, though indirectly, to the eternal 'Word'. Why it is seen as referring to this 'Word', and in what sense, will become clear in the course of the following two chapters when we discuss the nature of the unity which exists between Jesus and the 'Word'. Clearly if 'Jesus' can be seen as referring, even in this indirect way, in any meaningful sense to the eternal 'Word' of God, then, Jesus' unity with the 'Word' must be extraordinarily close and intimate indeed. We shall see that it is in fact an amazing unity.

This, it seems to me, is the obvious way to use the name 'Jesus'. When we think about it, we can see that it must, surely, have been the way in which the first disciples used it. There can hardly be any doubt that whenever they spoke about 'Jesus', the one to whom they were immediately and directly referring, and to whom they were understood to be referring, was the man from Nazareth whom they knew, and followed, and observed, and listened to – 'Jesus' was, we know, this man's name. When, later, Christians came to understand how intimately God was involved in the person and life and destiny of this carpenter and prophet from Nazareth, they came to see that the name 'Jesus', in referring to him, by that very fact, also necessarily referred to the eternal 'Son' or 'Word' of God who was so present in him. The name which referred immediately and directly to the human being, Jesus of Nazareth, was used, then, indirectly, of God's eternal 'Word'.

When we think about it in this way, it might come as a surprise to us to find that Walter Kasper, for example, finds it necessary to go to the trouble of acknowledging that this use of the name 'Jesus' is legitimate and within the bounds of orthodoxy: as long as we affirm the unity, the 'hypostatic' unity, which exists between Jesus and the eternal 'Word', using the name 'Jesus' to refer directly to the human being from Nazareth (this human 'nature') and indirectly to the eternal 'Word', is, Kasper says:

> ... more a question of theological usage and the ontology that it presupposes, and of christological approach, than a question of the binding doctrine of faith. Consequently the Church's magisterium has come to no decision in the matter (*Jesus the Christ*, p 240).

When, however, we recall the history of christology, we will not really be surprised at Kasper's concern. Throughout history there has been not only the perennial tendency to ignore the distinction between Jesus and God and, so, simply to identify Jesus with God, but also the Christian community's understandable fear of the opposite happening – that is, of Jesus and the eternal 'Word' being so separated that Jesus will then no longer be seen to be 'hypostatically' united to the eternal 'Word', and so not to be in any real sense, 'one and the same' as the eternal 'Word' (this, as is well known, was something which was perceived to have happened in 'nestorianism' to which we will refer at a later stage). However, this is a separation which, as Kasper points out, and as we shall see in the following chapters, is not at all necessarily entailed in using the name 'Jesus' in the way explained: it is no more necessarily entailed in our using the name in this way than it was in the early disciples' doing so.

A pastoral note

To conclude this chapter, some thought might be given to those who are still struggling to accept the Christian understanding of Jesus – to, for example, the many young searchers who are all around us today. For these, it seems to me, are not always dealt with as sympathetically as they might be, or helped as much as they deserve to be, in their efforts to come to understand and accept this Christian belief. Very often when one of these asks what Christians believe, or are expected to believe, about Jesus, they are immediately confronted with the statement 'Jesus is God'. Anyone, however, who has any perception at all of the radical difference which there is between Creator and creature (and enquirers today very often have such a perception) will know that to think of one who is human as being in any real sense God is a very difficult step to take. To *start* talking about Jesus in terms of his being God is, at its best, to start with a very advanced understanding of him indeed. It may very well, then, be saying too much too soon. 'Solid' believers, who are used to this way of talking about Jesus and who even take it for granted, need, today especially, to acknowledge how advanced their belief is and how difficult others may, understandably, find it to speak of any man or woman as being in any real sense God. There is a need today, more, perhaps, than formerly, to explore ways of helping others as gently as possible to move, gradually, towards this high point of Christian belief.

The faith-journey of the Christian community

In exploring such ways, some lessons can, I think, be learned from the history of the Christian community itself. For, we ought to remember, it was not only in terms of *being himself divine* that, throughout its history, the Christian community has thought and spoken about Jesus. In fact it is not only in these terms that even the scriptures speak about him. Indeed, the evidence is that it was not in these terms that the first Christians spoke about him. In all probability these arrived at this way of thinking and talking about him only gradually – that is, literally, step-by-step.

Already in Chapter Two I have pointed out that certain passages in, for example, the Acts of the Apostles and the Letters of Paul give us an insight into the way in which Jesus was first preached in the immediate post-resurrection period. We get this insight in, for example, the sermon, already referred to in Chapter Two, attributed to Peter on the first Pentecost. The way in which Peter talks about Jesus and his relationship with God in this sermon is worth commenting on in this context as it is both interesting and important. On this occasion Peter is represented as saying:

> ... Jesus the Nazarene was a man commended to you by God by the miracles and portents and signs that God worked through him when he was among you, as you all know. This man ... you took and had crucified ... You killed him, but God raised him to life, freeing him from the pangs of Hades ... God raised this man Jesus to life ... Now raised to the heights of God's right hand, he has received from the Father the Holy Spirit ... God has made this Jesus, whom you crucified, both Lord and Christ (Acts, 2: 22ff; *cf* 3: 11ff; 4: 8ff; 5: 29; 10: 40ff).

Peter's starting point here, we will note, is the man, Jesus of Nazareth – Peter starts 'from below'. But, we will also note, he proclaims this man Jesus, not in terms of one who is himself in any sense divine, but rather as a man in whom God is *acting and at work*.

That Peter should talk about Jesus in this way is understandable especially in the light of Israel's previous experience of God's involvement in their history. For, throughout their history, they had experienced God as *an active power* in their midst. In the experience of Exodus, for example, they were aware of God being moved by their suffering and act-

ing powerfully on their behalf – bringing them out of Egypt
'with mighty arm and outstretched hand', overcoming their
oppressors, rescuing them from their slavery and misery,
and leading them through the Sea and the desert into the
Promised Land. Accordingly, the evidence suggests that the
disciples first saw Jesus too, and what happened in him and
through him, in terms of a divine *action* in history: they saw
Jesus as another event in God's dealings with them. So, it
would appear, they proclaimed him, first of all, as one in
whom God was *active*.

They did not, of course, see Jesus as just one other event in
the long history of God's dealings with them. They came to
see him as one in whom God had acted 'in a unique and decisive way'. This, as I have pointed out in Chapter Two, was
partly because of what they had experienced God doing in
and through Jesus during his life, for, as Luke says, even
then they had been impressed

> ... by the things he (Jesus) said and did in the sight of
> God and of the whole people ... (Lk 24: 19).

They saw him as this 'decisive' or, as John Macquarrie likes
to put it, 'definitive', event in God's dealings with them
above all, of course, because of what they had experienced
God doing in his resurrection. For, in raising Jesus from the
dead, God had, they found, brought this man not just
through sea, as God had brought their ancestors of old, but
through death, and had exalted him to 'his own right hand'.
God had, then, brought Jesus, through that great final obstacle to human fulfilment, death, to New and Everlasting
Life. In doing this to and for a human being, God had, in
principle at least, rescued or 'redeemed' human life from
everything that threatens it. As John Knox, (a twentieth-cent-
ury scholar), has put it:

> Through this man – living, dying, risen – God brought
> into being a redeemed humanity' (*The Humanity and
> Divinity of Christ*, p 114).

In the resurrection of Jesus God had, in principle at least, brought humankind to completion and, in that sense had brought to its climax the divine creative work.

Learning from the past

Those of us who today would like to lead others to accept in its fullness the Christian community's belief in Jesus – or who would like to come to accept it ourselves – might learn two lessons in particular from this.

The first is that we should not be all that surprised if we find that for others, or indeed for ourselves, the journey towards acceptance, with conviction, of the Church's understanding of 'the divinity of Jesus' is a long one. The evidence suggests that it was a long one for the Christian community itself. To be able to say with conviction that a human being is in any real sense God, is, and always had to be, and always will be, a big and difficult step to take. It is a step which we might expect to come towards the end of a faith-journey rather than one which marks its beginning.

The second is that in trying to take this step, or in trying to help others to take it, it may not always be wisest to *begin* by thinking or talking in terms of Jesus being himself divine. The following might be a more gentle and helpful approach. We might first try to experience Jesus as one in whom – in his words and deeds and destiny – a 'Beyond' or divine power is at work in the world in an extraordinary way. We might try to experience him as the climax or, to use John Macquarrie's phrase, 'the high-water mark' of the divine involvement in the world. We might try to experience him as one who 'embodies' this 'Beyond' power in a unique way. If we could experience Jesus in this way, we might then be led more easily, and might more easily lead others – slowly and gradually, perhaps – to begin to think of him as one who can even be said to be *himself* in a real sense 'truly God'.

In what sense Jesus might himself be said to be 'truly divine' we shall discuss in the next two chapters.

'... the image of the unseen God'

(Col 1: 15)

If we are to do justice at all to the true Christian position regarding the relationship between Jesus and God we need a more nuanced statement than the simple one, 'Jesus is God'. At some level of understanding, every Christian knows this. Every Christian knows, for example, that, strictly speaking, Jesus is not thought of as being simply 'God', but, rather, as the 'Son' or the 'Word' of God. Every Christian also knows that, strictly speaking, Jesus is not even thought of as simply the 'Son' or 'Word' of God, but rather as 'the Son of God become a human being', 'the Word of God *become flesh*'. Deep down every Christian knows that the statement

'Jesus is the Word of God Incarnate'

is a much more accurate summary of Christian belief than the statement 'Jesus is God'.

Since this is so, if we are even to begin to appreciate how Christian faith really understands the unity between Jesus and God, in other words what 'the divinity of Christ' means, we need to try to understand what it means to speak of Jesus as 'Word' or 'Son' of God 'become a human being'. If we can begin to understand this, we will also begin, I believe, to see why Christian belief in Jesus as the climax of God's involvement in human affairs leads to a conviction about Jesus himself being divine.

'Trinity' – a note

It is easy to see that in using terms like 'Word' of God or 'Son' of God we are referring to what Christians call 'the Trinity'. The use of these terms in connection with Jesus reminds us that the Christian understanding of the relation between Jesus and God is in line with its understanding of God as 'Trinity'. We need, then, to refer at this point to the Christian notion 'Trinity'. We shall not examine this Christian insight in great detail in this book. Our interest here is the limited one of trying to understand Jesus as the 'Word' of God and it is this interest which will determine the aspects of Trinity which we shall highlight.

The Christian truth of the Trinity is often thought of as one which was revealed to the Christian community altogether 'from above', and which is believed altogether on blind faith. It should rather be seen as an expression of the Christian experience of God's presence in creation generally, and in Jesus and in the Church particularly.

Unity in diversity
For Christians at least, the word 'God' refers to what they encounter as, and what they believe to be, *really ultimate*. They understand Ultimate Reality to be profoundly single – in other words, they believe God to be *one*. This only makes good sense: for since the word 'God' refers to what is really Ultimate, to regard even two realities as gods, and, so, to speak of even two gods, would, in Christian terms at least, be a contradiction: neither 'god' would then really be Ultimate and, so, would not be at all what Christians call 'God'.

The God of Christian experience is, however, also unimaginably rich and diverse and complex, as any reflection on God's presence in creation as a whole, and in Christ and in the life of the Christian community in particular, will show. In general terms, it is this unity of God, consisting as it does in richness and diversity, which underlies the notion of Trinity. John Macquarrie puts it well in the following passage:

> As Ian Ramsey acutely observes, the Christian could not get along with the single word 'God' as his key word. A richer and fuller experience of deity demanded a more complex symbol for its expression. The Christian could

not go along with a stark monotheism ... but still less
with a pluralism like that of the world of polytheism with
its 'many gods and many lords' ...

Thus we may say that the doctrine of the Trinity tries to
elucidate the picture of God as he appears in the biblical
narrative and in the history of the Christian community.
He is a God who embraces diversity in unity, who is both
transcendent and immanent, who is dynamic and yet has
stability (*Principles of Christian Theology*, pp 191-2).

'Word' and 'Son'

What Christians are attempting to say when they speak of
Jesus as 'Word' and 'Son' begins to become clear when we
consider what these terms mean in everyday life.

'Word' is the term we usually use for that in which we express ourselves. So, we talk of the spoken or written word,
and even of the silent word which a gesture, like a nod, is.
'Word' is, then, a broad term covering every form of *self-
expression*.

'Son', of course, has to do with the phenomenon of reprod-
uction, whereby beings 're-produce' themselves. It refers to
the male human offspring which is the one to which some
more primitive communities were more likely to refer when
speaking of human offspring. For our purposes here, however, we can take 'son' as referring to *human offspring*.

We can see that the concept 'son' is not at all unconnected
with the broad concept 'word'. 'Son', understood broadly
as 'human offspring', also has to do with self-expression,
for offspring can be regarded as a really human, living
'word' in which people creatively express themselves. In
what follows I shall concentrate on Jesus as 'Word' of God
made flesh and, so, on the first of the two terms referred to.
If we can have some insight into what it means to call Jesus
'Word' of God made flesh, we will easily enough begin to
see what it means to call him 'Son' of God made flesh.

Creation as God's Word Incarnate

It seems to me that it is simply impossible to understand Jesus as the Word of God Incarnate without also, indeed first, seeing *creation as a whole* as a word of God incarnate. We will consider this in three stages and under three headings.

1. A created 'word' of God

God, being what is really ultimate, is the Source of all created being. God is, then, *Being,* from which, or from whom, all the created beings come and in which all their being is grounded.

God does not, as John Macquarrie puts it, 'hoard Being within himself'. Rather God 'pours out being' and gives being to the beings: God, or *Being,* in other words, is gracious. We can think, then, of God's act of creating as God 'expressing' outside Self, in creaturely terms, the Being which God is. In so far as we might think of God as *Source* or *Origin* of this creative act of expressing, we might think of God as 'Father', to refer to the term traditionally used by the Christian community. Using this exclusively male term for God naturally causes serious problems for many today: God, after all, is no more male than female but includes in divine Being both male and female in a transcendent way. It is important, therefore, that in what follows we use other images also to express this aspect of God.

With regard to the notion of God expressing divine Being outside Self, here, as all through this and the following chapter, the example of the creativity of a human artist will be found helpful. For in his or her creative activities the human artist too is really giving some form of outside expression to the being which she or he has and is within. Like the human activity of painting or writing, God's creative activity can be seen as an expression outside God of the Being which God is.

If God's act of creating can be seen in this way, then creation itself, which is that in which God expresses Self outside Self, can easily enough be thought of as a created 'word' of God. Furthermore, if we think of creation as giving 'body' or 'flesh' to God's Self-expression, we can even think of it as an embodiment or, to use the term broadly, as an 'en-fleshment' of the divine Self-expression. To echo the Latin word for flesh, *caro*, we can see creation as God's word 'in-carnate'. All created things, therefore, mirror God, image God, express God, 'en-flesh' and, in that sense, *'in-carnate'* God.

2. A created extension of God's Inner Word

The created 'word' of God can be seen as a created extension outside God of the Self-expressing which goes on eternally within God – that is, of God's *Eternal* Word. Here again the example of the painting or the poem is helpful. These too can be seen as expressions outside the artist of a dynamism towards self-expressing which is within the artist. Without this inner dynamism to express, the artist would never begin to express herself externally on canvas or in verse. This inner dynamism, which is, in fact, part of what the artist is, is what accounts for the outside 'word' which the artist utters. Somewhat similarly, we might think of the dynamic richness which Christians believe is characteristic of God, as being, to some extent at least, a dynamism towards Self-expression. We can think of God *eternally* expressing Self within divine Being. Again, somewhat as in the case of the human artist, we might think that it is this inner divine dynamism that accounts for God expressing Self outside, in created terms. In that sense, creation can be seen as a created extension outside of God of that Word uttered eternally within God – as a created expression of the Eternal Word of God. In creation, then, God speaks outside the Godhead and utters a *created* word about Self. In creation God 'speaks *out*'.

To 'complete', if only very briefly indeed, an outline of the Christian notion of Trinity, we might reflect further on the idea of an artist expressing self and, so, introduce at this point the Christian insight into God as 'Holy Spirit'. If we could think of there being an interaction between the artist, or any creative person, and that in which he or she expresses self – something which we can easily do in the case of a parent and a child – we might begin to see why Christians speak of God as 'Holy Spirit'. Christians have experienced that between Jesus and the Source of his being ('Father'), and between this Source and the Christian community, and indeed between creation and God as Source of its being, there is an interaction: they have experienced that there is, as it were, a loving force or dynamism linking and uniting them. As Christians see it, this relation between Artist and created 'word' reflects something which exists eternally between Artist and the eternal uncreated 'Word' within God – here once again, Christian belief sees what happens outside God as being a created extension of something within God. So, in the Christian view, it is not just Self-expressing which characterises the dynamism and richness which God is, but also a reaching out in mutual love and embrace. It is to this latter that Christian belief refers when it speaks of God as 'Holy Spirit'. In broad and very simple terms 'God the Holy Spirit' refers to divine Being in so far as this is characterised by a mutual reaching out, in loving embrace, uniting Artist and 'Word', 'Father' and 'Son'.

3. Creation – a revelation of God

It is important to note that, being a word which God utters, creation must also be seen as revealing something of God's inner being. For the word which a 'speaker' utters, no matter what form it takes, always reveals something of the being of the one who utters it. The painting or the poem, for example, in manifesting the capacity of the artist to think and to imagine and to compose creatively, and in giving access to her very inner thoughts and imaginings, reveals something of the inner being of the artist even to those who never met the artist face-to-face. God's creating activity, then, is also, automatically, a revealing activity: God's word of creation is also a word of revelation. Thus all created things, because they are a word uttered by God, mirror God and are, in their own way, an 'image' of God'. As the psalmist says

The heavens proclaim the glory of God

– a thought expressed by so many other poets also. Of course, we might observe in passing, anybody who looks at creation in any objective way will see that 'the glory of God' proclaimed by nature is indeed strange and enigmatic. Side-by-side with astonishing beauty and happiness and joy, even at times inextricably linked with these, there exists, both in the world of nature and of people, suffering and pain and, as we at least see and experience it, ugliness. Nobody who looks at creation in any objective way needs to be told that *Being*, as disclosed there, is indeed awesome and mysterious.

Created things mirror God in different ways and, according to the sophistication of their being, in varying degrees. Nowadays particularly we are conscious of the fact that the dividing line between the different grades of created being is not as sharp as we might have once thought. Allowing for this, we can say, nonetheless, that obviously-living things, like plants, express, for example, God's vitality in a way that apparently-lifeless things, like stones, do not; obviously-conscious living beings, like animals, express God's being in a way that apparently-unconscious living beings, like plants, do not; and self-conscious living beings, that is, human beings who can reflect on themselves, and are able to think and to love, are alone capable of expressing the thinking and loving character of God.

It is in the light of this understanding of creation as being in a real sense a word which God utters and, so, 'a word of God incarnate' and a word which reveals God, that we ought to understand that Incarnation of God's Word which the Christian community believes Jesus to be.

We shall consider Jesus as God's Word Incarnate in two closely connected stages – stage one in the remainder of this chapter and stage two in the following one. It ought to be noted, however, that it is only at the end of the second stage that we will have reached the heart of the Christian understanding of Jesus.

Jesus is '… the image of the unseen God …' (Col 1:15)

In the Christian view, when 'the fullness of time' came, God, who had always been expressing Self, expressed Self in created terms *as fully as possible* and, in Karl Rahner's phrase, 'with the utmost truth'. Since human beings, being free and able to love, can mirror God in a way that other created beings cannot, this fullest possible divine Self-expression necessarily took place in a human life – it necessarily took place in that human 'word' which a human being, or, a 'son', in the sense explained above, is. It necessarily took place in the most perfect, most complete human life – it necessarily took place in a *loving* 'son'. It resulted, Christians believe, in Jesus of Nazareth, in his words and in his works, in his death and, above all, in his destiny, that is, in his resurrection and exaltation. Here God had brought a human being and a human life to completion and fulfilment and, so, had, in principle at least, brought humankind to completion. God had here brought to a climax the divine creative work. Jesus, then, being in Christian experience the 'high-water mark' of God's involvement in creation, is for Christians the climax of God's *Self-expression in created terms*, and is, in this supreme way, *God's own 'Son' incarnate.*

Jesus is God's Word made flesh in a unique sense basically, therefore, because, in Christian experience, he is the Eternal Word of God now translated as accurately, as perfectly, and as fully as possible in created terms, in terms of a human life; he is the Eternal Word of God now become flesh 'with the utmost truth'. He is God's 'last word' about God. He is this, not, of course, in the sense that God ceased speaking after uttering the Word which Jesus is, but in the sense that, being, in Christian experience, the high-point of God's involvement in the world, he is for Christians God's *perfect* Word about God.

Since Jesus is the perfect Word, of God and about God, he is God's *living* Word, God's 'Son' incarnate, the 'Son' in whom God is 'well pleased'. Being God's perfect Word, he is the one most 'possessed by' and 'filled with' that unifying force of love which 'the Spirit' is.

Seeing Jesus as God's Word Incarnate in this sense, enables us to appreciate, even at this stage, three points in particular about the Incarnation and its significance.

Incarnation in context

It enables us to appreciate, first, that the Incarnation ought not to be seen as coming into human history like a 'bolt from the blue', having no context in creation or in history. Though a unique event, it is not an isolated one. It is the culmination of an age-long process. As the Irish theologian, Dermot A. Lane, puts it:

> The incarnation of Wisdom/Logos in Jesus is the coming into full glow of a cosmic process of divine self-communication set in motion millions upon millions of years ago. The Incarnation, therefore, is not some isolated divine intrusion that took place at one moment two thousand years ago but is rather the culmination and crystallisation of a divine cosmic process initiated at the dawn of time. The Incarnation was 'first' in God's intention – but not in time (*Christ at the Centre* , p 154).

This, of course, has important implications for the Christian's attitude to creation or, to use a contemporary term, 'the environment'. The Christian who reveres Jesus because he is God's Word, and who also sees him as being in continuity with what has been, and still is, taking place throughout the whole of creation, will immediately see that consist-

ency requires that reverence be shown also to creation generally. The Christian, seeing the manner and extent of God's
Self-expression in Jesus as being different from, and as sur-
passing, anything which is found elsewhere, will revere
Jesus accordingly. Nonetheless, seeing creation also as a
'word' uttered by God and, so, as embodying God, he or
she will see it too as worthy of great respect and reverence.
This, of course, applies also to history and the cultures and
religions which have emerged throughout history. Though
Jesus is, in the Christian view, God's 'last word' about God,
he is not at all the only word uttered by God throughout history.

'A new and radiant vision ...'
The understanding of Jesus as Word given above enables us
to appreciate, secondly, something of the significance of
Jesus for human life. God is invisible and, as we see when
we look around us, incomprehensible. Since God is what is
really ultimate, the great human question must be: what is
God like? It is expressed in John's gospel by Philip: 'Lord,
let us see the Father and then we shall be satisfied' (14:8).
The Christian view is that if we want to see what the mysterious, enigmatic God is like in *our* language, in *our* terms,
in *our* human situation, we look above all to Jesus of Nazareth. In other words, Christians believe that our best clue to
what Ultimate Reality is like is found in Jesus of Nazareth
and that we best understand that enigmatic and incomprehensible Ground of Being by looking at what happened in
and through this man. So, Jesus' reply to Philip was: 'To
have seen me is to have seen the Father' (14:9). Jesus is, in
the words of John A. Robinson, 'a window into God at
work'. The phrase 'at work' is important. We do not see
God in Jesus in the physical appearance of this man (the
gospels do not trouble about giving any description at all of
this). Nor is it particularly in Jesus' maleness that we see
God; as Brian O. McDermott says:

That Christ was male is a fact of his humanity as an indiv-

idual; the individual must possess a gender ... The tradition did not make Jesus's maleness (or Jewishness, or his
being a person of the first century c.e.) a principle of salvation, whereas it vigorously made his human nature, as
rooted in the divine Word and anointed by the Spirit, a
principle of salvation (*Word Become Flesh*, p 203).

This, McDermott rightly points out, is not to say 'that sex-
uality is not an extremely important dimension of our
humanity' (and, therefore, I might add, of Jesus' humanity
if we really take this seriously) '... but it does mean that, *sot-
eriologically* (that is, in terms of his function as Word Incarnate), Jesus' sex was not important' (p 243 – explanatory
words within brackets mine).

We see God in Jesus rather in his message and his ministry,
in his life and in his sufferings and, above all, in his death-
leading-to-the-resurrection-exaltation. We might recall that
the message and the ministry of Jesus is one of forgiveness
and love, and that in the resurrection of Jesus a human being is brought through death and, so, in the end, is made
victorious. It is through these – and they all have to do with
love and the liberation of people – that we see 'God at work'
or, in more biblical terms, God 'reigning'. If 'theology', in
the literal sense of the word, means 'a word about God',
then, as Karl Rahner says:

> Christology is the theology which God himself has
> taught, by speaking out his Word, as our flesh, into the
> void of the non-divine and sinful (*Theological Investig-
> ations*, vol 4, p 117).

It is this thought, or one very similar to it, that the Preface of
the Christmas Mass expresses, and it is for this aspect of the
Incarnation in particular that it invites us to give thanks
when it says (or sings):

> In the wonder of the incarnation
> your eternal Word has brought to the eyes of faith
> a new and radiant vision of your glory.

> In him we see our God made visible
> and so are caught up in love of the God we cannot see.
> And so, with all the choirs of angels in heaven
> we proclaim your glory ...

But even in Jesus and his love and liberating activity – indeed particularly in Jesus – we encounter again the enigmatic and awesome character of the God revealed in creation generally. The story of Jesus too is full of paradox: there power is exercised through weakness, success is achieved through failure, life is gained through suffering and death, victory through defeat.

A perspective on life
Seeing Jesus in this way opens up for us, thirdly, a new perspective within which we might view our own lives with all their incompleteness and ambiguities and struggle. These are aspects of our lives which, naturally, we experience as burdensome. Consequently we are often tempted to see them as some sort of a mistake, as a lot which, really, ought not be ours, and we wish they would go away. Here a point developed by Karl Rahner is worth noting. That which resulted when God uttered his most perfect Word about Self, was a human life, the life of Jesus of Nazareth. Even though this life of Jesus was a particular human life, it was, nonetheless, a real human life with all the incompleteness, and ambiguities and struggle which necessarily go with human living: being '... tempted in every way that we are ...', Jesus too '... offered up prayer and entreaty, aloud and in silent tears' during his life (Heb: 4:15; 5:7). Human life itself, and not just the life of Jesus, is a word uttered by God about God. As such it mirrors God and the mystery which God is:

> If God wills to become non-God, man comes to be, that and nothing else, we might say ... man is for ever the articulate mystery of God ... He is a mystery which partakes for ever of the mystery on which it is founded (Karl Rahner, as above, p 116-7).

Even the limitedness and the ambiguity and the struggle of our own lives, ought not, then, be viewed simply as the result of the 'Adam'-sin in the past. If looked at in the light of the Incarnation, these aspects of our lives too might be seen as in some way mirroring the mystery which God is and, so, as giving us some insight into this enigmatic, incomprehensible God. Seeing them in this way might alert us to the risk of having too narrow and earth-bound a concept of that divine 'glory' of which the life of Jesus gives us 'a new and radiant vision'. Such a narrow and earth-bound concept often emerges when we are faced with the suffering and evil which are so much a part of God's creation and of our own lives.

* * *

Seeing Jesus as the Word of God translated as perfectly as possible in terms of a human life, enables us to see more clearly than was possible in the previous chapter why precisely the statement 'Jesus is God' is a poor summary of Christian belief. The whole point of Jesus is that he is a *translation* of the Word of God in created terms, or, better, a created embodiment or *en-fleshment* of this Word. In other words, the whole point of the Incarnation is that it is an incarnation! We can only properly understand Jesus, then, when we see him as God's Word in *human terms,* or, to use the more traditional phrase, as the '*Incarnate* Word of God'. The statement 'Jesus is God' does not refer to the idea of incarnation at all. It is precisely because it makes no reference whatsoever to what God's self-utterance in Jesus is really all about that it is such an unsatisfactory summary of Christian belief regarding Jesus. More nuanced statements like: 'Jesus is God's Word in created terms', or 'Jesus is God's Word in human terms', or (to return to the traditional language) 'Jesus is the Word of God Incarnate', do refer to the Incarnation and, so, are much more accurate summary-statements.

As such, they are also less confusing: these, at least, do not give the impression, and cannot be interpreted as implying, that Christian belief simply equates a human, created, being with God, or, in other words, that it simply equates a being with *Being*.

CHAPTER TEN

Divine Self-Portrait in flesh

To say that Jesus is the perfect created Word of God might seem to be saying too little about him and to be doing little justice to the Christian conviction regarding this man. There is, however, more to saying that Jesus is God's perfect created Word than, perhaps, might meet the eye. It will help us to see this if we focus on a familiar enough image – that is, that of an artist creating a self-portrait. Focusing on this will, I believe, help us to understand more fully the Christian conviction regarding the uniqueness of Jesus.

Two artists

We might think, first, of a *human* artist choosing to 'reproduce' himself through a medium which is other than himself: we might think of him – or her – choosing to create *A Self-Portrait in Oils*. And we might think of him as producing a masterpiece. Of course when the artist sets out on such a project, he chooses to be limited in his self-expression by the limitations inherent in the chosen medium. Thus neither he himself, nor any sane person, would dream of considering the self-portrait defective because, for example, it is only two-dimensional and is unable to talk or walk and, so, does not match the level of being which the artist himself has. Within the limits of the chosen medium he might well, however, produce a masterpiece of self-portraiture.

Somewhat similarly we might think of God as the divine artist who chooses to express and reproduce Self through a medium which is other than Self: we might think of God setting out to create God's *Self-Portrait In Flesh*. We might further think of God as creating through this medium the perfect self-portrait. Here again we need to remember that

God, though exploring new creative possibilities in choosing this medium, also decides to be limited by the constraints which the medium necessarily imposes. The divine Self-portrait will, then, be a self-portrait in 'flesh', that is, in human life. To be disappointed that this divine Self-portrait is only of human dimensions and that it cannot do everything which the artist can do, would of course, be absurd: it would be to forget the whole point of self-portraiture and would be like being disappointed because Van Gogh's self-portrait cannot talk! If we think of Jesus as this divine Self-portrait, then we can speak of him as God's perfect *Self-Portrait In Flesh*.

Thinking of Jesus in this way deepens our appreciation of him as one in whom God reveals the divine Being. For, in terms of revealing something of the artist, a self-portrait always has a value which many other forms of self-expression do not have. In creating a self-portrait, no artist sets out to give us a 'photograph' of himself as seen from the outside. Rather he starts out, of set purpose, to express and to reveal, in as creative a way as possible, how he sees and experiences himself: in a self-portrait, somewhat as in an autobiography, the artist sets out to tell his own story. If we see Jesus as God's *Self-Portrait in Flesh*, we will, then, see him as one in whom God manifests, creatively, how God sees and experiences Self. We will see him as one in whom we are given not just an outsider's view of God, but, rather – amazingly – an insight into what it is like for *God* to be God. The implications of this are, I think, something which the reader might ponder as she or he reflects on the message and ministry and life of Jesus. The reader might reflect, for example, on such features of Jesus' ministry as his emphasis on service rather than lordship, his empathy with the poor, the downtrodden, the weak and the wounded, his vulnerability, his suffering and his death, and ponder what these might possibly – and, again, amazingly – be saying about God's experience of being God. Jesus, we know, had a name for mixing with a certain type of people – the type with whom the 'pious' and 'respectable' ones would not like to be associated: he was, these latter said,

> … a friend of tax collectors and sinners (Mt 11: 19).

He was one who

> … welcomes sinners and eats with them (Lk 15: 1).

A saying which we often hear used comes to mind here: 'Tell me your company and I will tell you who you are'. It might be said regarding Jesus: 'Tell me your company and I will tell you who *God* is'!

Portraits with a difference

In the Christian view, there is, of course, one particularly important difference between the self-portrait of the human artist and that which God creates in Jesus of Nazareth.

In the case of the human portrait, while it owed its existence to the artist in the first place, afterwards it remains completely distinct from her or him. Now at least it has its own separate existence. Consequently, its subsequent history – in art galleries, in auction rooms, on walls, in attics – is *its* history alone.

As the Christian community sees it, the relation between God's Self-portrait, Jesus of Nazareth, and the divine artist is very different. We shall reflect on this in two stages. We shall first state what, in the everyday language of faith, this difference is, and then we shall see how we might try to have some understanding of it.

Stating the belief

Stating in the everyday language of faith *what* the difference is believed to be, is something we need to do calmly – for the conviction in question is, indeed, an amazing one.

In the case of the divine Self-portrait, as is well known to Christians, artist and portrait are believed not to have gone their different ways. In fact they are believed to be forevermore inseparably united in an unprecedented and unparalleled way. In creating this Self-portrait, the divine artist is believed to have created an extension of Self to the extent of finding in it a new way of being and living – a created way of being and living. The artist is believed to be now living and moving in and through this extension of Self in such a way that the life and history of the Self-portrait is, so it is believed, the human life and the human history of the artist. So much is the portrait believed to be an extension of the Being of the artist, that Christians see whatever happens to the portrait as happening also to the artist of whose being it is a real extension! So, in the pain of Jesus, they see God*self* suffering – suffering, that is, in the sufferings of this created extension of the divine Self, this created divine Self-portrait; in the tears of Jesus, they see God*self* weeping – weeping, that is, in the tears of this created extension of the divine Self, this created Self-portrait; in the death of Jesus they see God*self* taking on and experiencing our mortality – experiencing it, that is, in the mortality of this created extension of the divine Self, this created Self-portrait; in the resurrection of Jesus they see God*self* experiencing victory over human mortality – experiencing it again in the victory of this created extension of the divine Self, this created divine Self-portrait. And because they believe that, in an ultimate sense, the life of Jesus is the human life of the Eternal Word, Christians believe that whatever can be said about the portrait, Jesus, can also be said about the Eternal Word of God. So, to take what is perhaps the best known example of this, they believe that Mary, who is the mother of Jesus of Nazareth, is also, by that very fact, the mother of the Eternal Word of God in his created existence – they believe that she is, in traditional language, the mother of the Word of God Incarnate.

Several times already we have encountered something of the paradoxical nature and the subtlety of Christian belief:

Jesus, we have seen, cannot be understood as divine unless he is taken seriously as human; the unity which exists between him and God cannot be understood unless the distinction between them is appreciated; even God's own inner unity cannot be understood without reference to the diversity of which belief in the Trinity speaks. Here once again we come up against paradox and subtlety: this time in the context of God's unchanging character. In the Christian view, God, *Ultimate Reality*, is, and remains, stable, unchangeable, immutable. But, in this view, God also really *became* in the Incarnation. As Karl Rahner says:

> ... we learn from the incarnation that immutability (which is not eliminated) is not simply and uniquely a characteristic of God, but that in and in spite of his immutablility *he* can truly *become* something. He himself, he, in time (*Theological Investigations*, vol 1, p 114, note 3).

The subtlety of the Christian position regarding the unchangeability of God is expressed well by Rahner:

> If we face squarely the fact of the Incarnation, which our faith testifies to be the fundamental dogma of Christianity, we must simply say: God can become something, he who is unchangeable in himself can himself become subject to change in something else (*Theological Investigations*, vol 4, p 113).

We can hardly be surprised – any more than Rahner is – that, when faced with the fact of the unchangeable God actually *becoming* in the Incarnation,

> ... the traditional philosophy of the schools begins to blink and stutter (as above, p 113).

Attempting to make sense of the belief
How might we try to understand and make sense of the Christian belief regarding the relationship between Jesus and God, between artist and portrait, described above?

It must be said at the outset that since there is question here of what is believed to be the unequalled high-point of God's involvement in history, we have now moved beyond the ordinary and the everyday and the familiar and reached the edges of Christian and human experience: the unity which Christians see existing between Jesus and God is, to use Karl Rahner's words again, 'such as is not found elsewhere and remains profoundly mysterious'. Being different from anything else in our experience, the Incarnation will, then, always remain, to some extent at least, beyond our grasp.

Having said this, we must also hasten to say that this does not mean that we can make no sense at all of this Christian belief and that, accordingly, this must always appear to us as non-sense. Unique though the Jesus-event is, it is nonetheless an event of divine creativity. Creativity, however, is something of which we do have direct, even though limited experience – limited, that is, relative to God's creativity. It is this human experience of creativity which, it seems to me, best provides us with a key to understanding the Christian conviction regarding Jesus, and it is in linking with this experience that our best hope of making sense of the Incarnation lies. We need, then, to reflect further on our own experience of creativity, focusing now on our creative activity as attempts to express ourselves.

Ex-pression

The derivation of the word 'expression' is a good starting point here as it draws our attention to an aspect of self-expression which might easily escape our notice. The word comes from two Latin words which together mean 'a pressing out'. This serves to remind us that in all our efforts at self-expression what we are really doing is 'pressing out' ourselves. We are, in these efforts, 'pressing out' the being that is within us, giving it some form of existence outside us, and, so, extending outside us the being that we are. So, the artist and the author, the cabinet-maker and the cook, when they express themselves in their respective ways, 'press out' the being which they themselves have and are, and, out of it, give being to their creation. And indeed it is very interesting to note that we often say of these that they 'put themselves into' their work. Regarding that in which we express ourselves, that is, our 'word' in the broad sense, the derivation of 'expression' reminds us that this, be it a book or a painting, a cabinet or a dish, begins to exist in the first place only because it participates in our own being. As an embodiment outside us of the being that is within us, it is, then, in a sense an extension of ourselves. Thus, again interestingly, we often say – and indeed rightly – of the creation into which we have poured our being: 'There is a lot of me in that'. If it is a creation in which we have been particularly intensely involved, we might even say: 'I have put my *all* into that'. Since the act of expressing self always is an act of 'pressing out' self and, so, of extending self, we can see that to the extent to which we really do succeed in expressing ourselves, we also succeed, to that extent, in putting ourselves into our self-expression. We can see too that, conversely, it is to the extent to which we do succeed in putting ourselves into the 'word' which we 'utter' (whatever form it takes) that our 'word' really is our *self*-expression. It is for this reason that the child, into whose rearing (and not just begetting) parents creatively put so much, can truly be said to be their living 'word' in a special sense.

Limits to divine creativity?

We need to recall again at this point how the Christian conviction regarding Jesus arises. It arises, as I have pointed out in earlier chapters, out of the Christian experience of Jesus. Specifically it arises out of the experience of the intensity of the divine activity in him, in his life, his ministry, his death and, above all, his resurrection and glorification, and his continued influence, as the Risen One, in the Christian community. Since Christian faith understands Jesus to be the high-point of God's involvement in history, it believes that God was, and is, as involved in this human life as God could possibly be in a single human life. We might say, then, that, in the Christian view, God has put God's 'all' into this human life and history and eternal destiny, into this creation. The extent to which even a human artist succeeds in putting his 'all' into his creation, and the very real sense in which which he may be able to say of his work, 'There is a lot of me in that', is, as we know, considerable. Still, it is, of course, very limited. It is, for example, only in a very loose sense that we can say that the history of Van Gogh's self-portrait really is his own personal history.

Reflection on our own creativity – on our own success at 'pressing out' our being, extending it outside ourselves, and putting ourselves, our 'all', into our creations – can lead us to reflect on God's creative possibilities. God is not a human artist, but Creator. Human creativity is only a pale reflection of the Creator's creativity. Our own experience might, then, enable us to think of God as *so* 'pressing out' the divine Being, as *so* putting Self into this creation, Jesus, as to have succeeded in expressing Self here in a way that a human artist might wish to do but cannot – not even if the human artist had the intensity and passion and creativity of a Michelangelo saying 'Speak!' to his statue of Moses. In other words, in the light of our own sometimes consider-able creative achievements, we might think of God as exer-cising and achieving in Jesus the ultimate in creativity and self-expression.

If we could think of God in this way we would seem to be then thinking of God as expressing Self in Jesus in the way Christians believe. The aim of all self-expression is, as I have said, to 'press out' and extend our being. The measure of successful self-expression is the extent to which we really do succeed in putting ourselves into our creation. If that is so, then would not the *really perfect* created self-expression take place when the Self-portrait is that real extension of the artist's being which, Christians believe, Jesus is of the divine Being? The measure of the adequacy of the 'word' in which we express ourselves is, as I have also said, the extent to which it really does embody us. Again would not God's *perfect* created Word embody, in a created way, the divine Self in the way that Christians believe Jesus to embody the eternal divine Word? We cannot, of course, think of creatures, with their limited creative powers – their *created* creative powers – achieving such perfect self-expression. This, however, does not at all necessarily mean that we cannot think of the Creator, Creativity Itself, achieving it, as ought to become clearer when we discuss the idea of Creator in the next chapter.

Jesus as 'Son' of God Incarnate

In thinking about God as creating in the life and destiny of Jesus the perfect divine Self-portrait, we must take into account the fact that God did this, and could only have done it, through the free cooperation of Jesus. As we know, the intensity of the divine involvement in the life and destiny of Jesus did not mean that God manipulated Jesus in any way, or took anything away from his freedom as a human being before God: Jesus, no less than any other human being, we will recall, always had the shaping of his destiny in his *own* hands and was, no less than any other human being, the author of his *own* script for his own life.

Here we can see the value of seeing Jesus as the 'Son' Incarnate as well as the 'Word' Incarnate. To describe Jesus as a 'word' which God uttered might suggest that in Jesus God expressed Self in lifeless terms. The term Son, however, has the value of bringing out the fact that when God expressed Self perfectly it was in a loving Son who always responded, in complete freedom, to the Father's love, and that there always existed between Jesus and God that intimate personal relationship which appears so strikingly in the gospels and which is so commonly referred to in books and sermons about Jesus: Jesus and the 'Father', in other words, were perfectly united by that bond of unity which we call 'the Holy Spirit'. Thinking of Jesus as Son enables us, then, to see him not only as God's perfect Word uttered in and to creation, but as creation's perfect answer to that Word addressed to it by the Father.

Jesus: representative of the cosmos

In the Christian view, the Word of God has in Jesus taken as 'Its' very own, not an inert 'block' of humanity, but a human life and a human history. Indeed, in the Christian view, the Word of God may be seen to have taken as 'Its' own the history of the cosmos itself. Today, especially because of an evolutionary view of the cosmos, we are conscious of the great basic cosmic unity which exists. In such a cosmic view we see each stage of the evolutionary process as bringing with it, ennobled, the lower stage: we see matter itself becoming alive in plant life, becoming conscious in animal life, and becoming reflective, intelligent and free – self-conscious – in human life. We see the human being as a *microcosm* bringing together, ennobled, all the 'lower' stages of evolution – we see the human being, as has been said, as 'clay grown tall'. In the language of Dorothy Sölle, Jesus is 'The Representative'. He can be seen, however, as the representative, not just of the race but of the cosmos. In so far as he, no more than any other human being, is not an island, but is part of the vast cosmos, the history of the cosmos as a whole is his history. It is also, by that very fact, God's own history. In the Christian view, then, God is not an artist who creates a work of art and remains aloof from its history, standing serenely, as it were, outside it and indifferent as to its outcome. God is, rather, a Creator who, through Jesus, enters into the history of his creation. In the history of the cosmos, God's own history is now in question. This cosmic aspect of Jesus is one to which Pope John Paul II, for example, has referred:

> The Incarnation of God the Son signifies the taking up into unity with God not only human nature, but in this human nature, in a sense, of everything that is flesh ... The Incarnation, then, also has a cosmic significance, a cosmic

dimension: the 'first born of creation' unites himself in some way with the entire reality of man, within the whole of creation (*Dominum et Vivificatum*, no 50).

* * *

At first sight it might appear that to say that 'Jesus, in his words and his works, his death and his destiny, is the most God-like of creatures, the one who most reveals God', is to fall very short of the truth of the Christian conviction regarding him. On reflection, however, it can be seen that this statement, fully understood, contains that truth. For if we understand Jesus to be the most God-like of creatures because of the initiative which *God* first of all took in him, then we are saying that Jesus most reveals God because in him God most reveals the divine Self. We are then saying that Jesus is God's perfect created Self-expression. And if we understand *God's* perfect created Self-expression as that into which God poured out the divine being and put God's 'all', in a way that only the Creator could, then we are saying that Jesus is the eternal Word of God who is so filled with 'the fullness of God' (Col 2:9) as to be that real living extension of the divine Being described above. And if this is what we are saying when we say that 'Jesus is the most God-like of creatures, the one who most reveals God', we are really saying what the Christian community itself means when it says that in Jesus

The Word was made flesh,
he lived among us
(Jn 1: 14).

Concluding Questions

CHAPTER ELEVEN

Human or divine - A dilemma?

The Christian understanding of Jesus, even when properly understood, might indeed seem to be an impossible one to expect any intelligent person to accept. On the one hand, Christians insist that Jesus was a human being who was fully independent and fully free before God. On the other hand, they believe that he belonged to God as God's very own – so much so that his human life, though lived in freedom before the Word of God, was God's very own human life.

How, it might very reasonably be asked, could this possibly be? If Jesus so belonged to God, how could he then really belong to himself? Surely the more his life was the human life of the eternal Word of God, the less it was the free, independent life of the carpenter from Nazareth? In saying that Jesus was, on the one hand, human and, therefore, free and independent before God, and, on the other, divine, in that his life was the very human life of Godself, are we Christians not trying to have it both ways? Are we not caught in a dilemma? Have we not to say *either* that Jesus, like us all, was living a life which was free before God, *or* that, unlike us, he was living a life which was not his own, but God's?

The 'God or creature?' dilemma

This is a dilemma to which we need to give serious consideration. It is one which faces us, not just in this context, but continually in our attempts to make sense of our faith.

We meet it in connection, for example, with the Bible – as ought to be clear from what has been said already. On the one hand we believe that God was involved in the writing of the Bible, and was so involved in these books that, as Vatican II so starkly puts it,

> ... these have God as their author (*Dei Verbum*, 11).

On the other hand we believe that the human authors of these books are, again in the words of Vatican II, 'true authors':

> ... while employed by him (God) they made use of their own powers and abilities ... (as above).

So much are they the 'true authors' that,

> ... the interpreter of sacred Scripture, in order to see clearly what God wanted to communicate to us, should carefully investigate what meaning the sacred authors really intended ... (as above).

The human authors are, then, as truly the authors of their respective books as I am of this book or as the reader is of the last letter or other literary piece which he or she has written. If these books really '... have God as their author', how can the human authors really be their 'true authors' – one hundred per cent their authors? To the extent that God is really their author, surely, to that extent, the human authors are not really their authors?

The dilemma arises again in connection with a Christian's, or, indeed, any believer's, attitude to evolution. As one who listens to and learns from the discoveries and findings of science, the intelligent Christian is at least open to the evolutionary theory of the origin and development of the world: she or he is open to the possibility (to put it mildly) that 'lower' forms of being, of themselves, and out of their very own resources, *themselves* produce higher forms of being – that, for example, the 'lower' animals, of themselves and out of their own resources, *themselves* produced human life. As a believer, however, he or she believes that God was, and always is, deeply involved in this process in all its stages and phases, so much so that it is *God* who enables every level of life to produce the higher form. How, it might be asked again, can such a position be held? Surely if beings produce higher forms of themselves, then there is no place or need for God to give it to them to produce these? To the extent that it really is God who gives it to them to produce these higher forms, then, surely to that extent they do not produce them of *themselves*?

A third and final example which, in the light of present day experience is worth mentioning here, has to do with the Church's search for the truth. On the one hand, a Christian believes that the Spirit of Jesus is with the Church '… always, even to the end of the world' guiding it in its teaching of the truth. But on the other hand, every Christian knows, today especially, that the official teachers in the Church have to work very hard to understand the truth of revelation – so much so, in fact, that Vatican II makes the following statement about the duty of the Church's teachers to search out the truth:

> The Roman Pontiff and the bishops, in view of their office and of the importance of the matter, strive painstakingly and by appropriate means to inquire properly into that revelation … (*Lumen Gentium*, 25).

Once again it might be asked: if the Spirit of God is believed to be so involved in guiding the Church in the way of truth, why is it necessary for its official teachers to work so 'painstakingly' to reach that truth? Might it not be said that in so far as God is at work here, to that extent people are relieved of the work, and that, in so far as the Church is really a divine institution, to that extent it ceases to be a really human one?

The dilemma, 'either God or creature', 'either human or divine', which arises in a very obvious way in the context of Jesus, arises, then, in different ways in other contexts also. In fact, it arises in some form or other whenever we think about God's involvement in human affairs or indeed in creation generally. It is one which obviously needs serious consideration here.

When we do consider the dilemma seriously, we find that it turns out to be, not a real dilemma at all, but a false one. It is false because, ultimately, it arises out of a very false notion of God. That this is so can easily be seen if, at this point, we reflect a little on God as *Creator*: the notions of creation and creativity have emerged as very important in our discussion in the previous chapter of the relationship between Jesus and God.

Creation: Dependence and independence

That the word 'creation' refers to the origin of the universe is, of course, common knowledge. Even more particularly it is common knowledge that, for believers at least, 'creation' means that the universe and everything in it has its origin in God and exists only because God gives it the being which it has.

Very often, however, creation is thought of almost exclusively in terms of the divine action which brought the universe into being in the first place – 'in the beginning'. Accordingly, the word 'creation' is associated only with an event in the past. Once having brought the universe into being, and having, as it were, set it in motion, God is thought of as having ceased creating, God's creating activity being considered no longer necessary. The idea of God 'resting' after completing the work of creation still lurks somewhere in the unconscious.

It really takes only a little reflection to see that this is, of course, a very inadequate notion of creation. This becomes clear especially when we see creation in the way I suggested in Chapter Nine. There I spoke of creation in terms of Being, not hoarding, but sharing Being and giving a created participation in Being to beings. If we think of creation in these terms, then we are thinking of created beings as existing because, and in so far as, they are given this participation in Being – because, and in so far as, God 'utters' them. But if this is the case, the following rather startling conclusion follows: the difference between a creature and nothing consists entirely in what God gives to the creature; it consists entirely in the participation in Being which is given to the creature. This, I think, is what we always really meant when we said that God creates 'out of nothing'. In saying this we obviously did not mean to imply that God used 'nothing' as the material out of which God created things. We meant, rather, that God gives creatures their whole being, so that apart from what God gives them they are nothing. From this two points of particular relevance to our present study follow.

The first is that God's creating activity is just as necessary now as it was 'in the beginning'. For if God were to suspend the activity of giving beings the being which they have, the *whole* being which they have, (something which, of course, we could not imagine happening), the result would be the very same as if God had withheld this activity 'in the beginning'. The result would be *nothing* – nothing, that is, other than God (Being). So, the beings which came to be simply because 'in the beginning' God gave them their whole being, continue to be only in so far as God continues to give them their whole being – only in so far as God continues to 'utter' them.

The second point is that, contrary to what is often thought, the concept 'creation' does not at all refer primarily to origins, to a relationship which existed just at the start. It refers primarily to dependence and, therefore, to the present relationship between Creator and creature. In fact, the word creation, properly understood, only states this relationship. As Piet Schoonenberg puts it:

'Creation' does not add anything to the relation between God and the world – the word merely expresses the activity of this relation, it says that in this relation God is always the one who realizes (*i.e. gives reality to, real-izes*) the world in all its components and aspects and that on the other hand the world is completely and wholly realized by God, from God, and in God. (*The Christ*, p 22, italicised words mine).

When we think about it, we can see that it is, of course, *dependence* that we ourselves really affirm when we say that something is created. For when we say that something is created, we are saying that it is a creature or that it is creaturely. And when we say that it is a creature or is creaturely we are saying much more than that it came from God in the first place. We are saying that it is not the absolute foundation of its own being, that, rather, it derives its being, that *all* its being participates in Being (God) and, so, is given by Being, is grounded in Being and is supported by Being. We are talking, not so much about origins, as about a being's radical dependence for all of its being.

A paradox

These reflections on the notion of creation make it possible for us to appreciate something of the paradox which characterises the relationship between Creator and creature. We appreciate this when we take into account three very important facts.

The first is the one already mentioned, namely, that the being which we have is dependent: we have it only because it is now being given to us by God and only in so far as it is being given to us by God. The second is that this dependence does not make our being any less our own being: my being is still my own being. And the third is that it is precisely because our being is radically dependent on God that it is there at all and that it is ours at all: if we did not come from God and were not dependent on God, we simply would not exist at all.

The paradox, then, is that our total and radical dependence on God does not make us in any way less independent, free, individual, personal beings in the world. On the contrary, and paradoxically, it is precisely because, and in so far as, we are radically dependent on God that we are the independent, free beings which we are in the world! We have here, then, a relationship which is altogether different from, indeed is the very opposite of, all relationships within the world. In other relationships, to the extent to which we are really dependent on others, to that extent we are less independent. In our relationship with God, however, the opposite is the case: *we are independent and free precisely in so far as we are dependent!* As Karl Rahner puts it:

> The relationship between God and the creature is characterized, precisely in contrast to any causal dependence otherwise met with within the world, by the fact that self possession and dependence increase in direct, and not in inverse proportion (*Sacramentum Mundi*, 2. p 424).

Freedom in God

The paradoxical nature of the relationship between creator and creature emerges even more clearly when we consider one particular aspect of our created being, that is, our freedom – an aspect of human life which, of course, is very relevant to our present reflections on Jesus.

That we are, sometimes at least, in control of our own actions is clear from experience. We all know that, sometimes at least, we choose a certain course of action freely and of our very own accord. So much so, that we know that on these occasions it was we, and not anybody else, who made these choices and, so, we regard ourselves alone as responsible or answerable for these actions. We know that on these occasions we just cannot shift the blame on to, or give the credit to, someone else.

Yet, as creatures, we are *totally* dependent on God – dependent on God for all that we have and are and do. Creation means, then, that not only is the faculty of freedom given to us by God but – amazingly – that even our free actions, and – perhaps even more amazingly – even that which is most personal and free in our free actions, are given by God!

After all, nothing could exist, no element in even our free actions could exist, if it did not participate in Being and was not upheld by Being: the insight behind the notion of creation, we may not forget, is that everything other than God is dependent on God. (It is, of course, only when we appreciate this that we can begin to see the full dimensions of the problem of evil – a problem which is often, it must be admitted, dismissed by preachers and even theologians in too facile a manner. It is a problem which cannot, and indeed need not, be dealt with here; anyone who might wish to pursue the problem will find in the notes to this chapter some recommended reading. Enough to say here that, when honestly faced, the experience of evil can lead us to a more profound and richer understanding of God than we would otherwise have.) We are free, then. Yet even our free acts, and all the elements of our free acts, even that which is most personal in them, are given to us by God and are dependent on God. All *is* ours. Yet all is from God.

The paradoxical fact, however, is – and here the paradox appears in a very striking way – that the fact that our free actions, and the very free element in our free actions, are given to us by God, are upheld by God, and derive all their being from God, does not in any way make us less free and does not make these free actions less our very own free actions. Paradoxically, it is precisely because these actions, in all their elements, are given to us by God that they take place at all, that they are ours at all, and that they are free at all. All is ours *precisely* because all is from God!

The basis of the paradox

How might we at all account for this radical difference in relationships? The explanation is to be found, simply but profoundly, in the radical difference which there is between Creator and creatures, between Being and the beings.

That God is different from any created reality is something we all know. We know, for example, that God is beyond our comprehension and that we cannot at all imagine what God is like. We find ourselves able to say things about God that we could not possibly say about creatures. So, we say, for example, that God is everywhere and nowhere – everywhere, in the sense that God is always present giving being to everything that is; nowhere, in the sense that God does not occupy space or place at all. We know well that God is different.

How different God is, however, is something which we often seriously underestimate. We may think that we regard God as radically different from everything else. But when all is said we really think of God as being only a lot different from everything else. An experience which I have often had in connection with one of the stories from Anthony de Mello's beautiful book, *The Song of the Bird*, will illustrate this.

The story in question is the one about the elephant and the rat. The elephant is bathing in a pool and the rat, from the bank, is insisting that he get out. After a while, due to the rat's persistence, the elephant does reluctantly lumber out and asks the rat why he wanted him to get out of the pool. 'To check if you were wearing my swimming trunks', said the rat. The moral which is added to the story is:

> An elephant will sooner fit into the trunks of a rat than God into our notions of him (*The Song of the Bird*, p 7).

This story, I find, as well as amusing people, also impresses them deeply. After hearing the story, people seem to lapse into silent reflection on the mystery that is God. They are often surprised, however, and somewhat taken aback, when I point out that, when all is said, the story really does little justice to the difference which there is between God and creatures – that, in fact, in this respect the story can be misleading. For when we think about it, we can see that the story is really presenting God as another creature – massively bigger, of course, than other creatures, but still a creature. After all, as far as wearing swimming trunks is concerned, the only difference between an elephant and a rat is one of proportions: it consists mainly in the fact that the elephant is massively bigger.

This story seems to me to typify the way in which people often think about God. Despite what they say about God being different from creatures, despite even their use of words like 'infinitely' to describe the extent of this difference, they still think of God as being, not radically different, but just a lot different from creatures: they really think of God, surprising as it may seem, in terms of another creature, 'infinitely' bigger than other creatures, but still a creature. So, they find themselves saying such things as *'either* God *or* creatures'*: they argue, for example, 'either my free action comes from me or it comes from God'; they argue as though God and creatures were on the same level.

God, of course, is not a creature. God's being – and God's alone – is not created at all. God is Creator. Being Creator, God creates. God gives being and upholds being and supports it. Everything else receives being and is created. God, then, is not just a lot different from creatures. Despite the fact that creatures are a 'word' uttered by God and, so, mirror God, and that the human creature is in a special sense made to the image and likeness of God, God is still radically different from creatures. No greater difference is possible. It is, of course, because of this radical difference that we find ourselves saying, for example, that God is everywhere and nowhere. What we are really saying is that God, being Creator, transcends all such creaturely categories. We are saying, in other words, that God is *transcendent* – a point, I might add, of which Anthony de Mello too was, of course, very much aware and which he brings out beautifully so often in his writings and in his stories; the reader might see, for example, the title story of the book referred to above.

A false dilemma

It is because of this radical difference between God and

creatures that the simple 'either X or Y' dilemma does not apply here. Such rivalry or opposition or mutual exclusion does apply when there is question of beings of the same order acting on the same level and in the same way. Thus we can, and must, say of two human authors, like Peter and Paul, that to the extent that Peter is the true author of a book, Paul cannot, to that extent, be the true author: Paul's authorship role would exclude Peter's since both would be of the same kind.

If, however, we have any appreciation at all of what it means to say that God is Creator, we can see that this simple dilemma 'either God or creature' does not at all apply. For since God is radically different from creatures, God's way of being present and active is radically different from a creature's way of being present and active. God's presence in creatures is always a *creating* presence. It is the presence in them of Being. Far from taking away from the creature's own being, it is, of course, precisely this which actually provides the creature with a being of its very own. Equally God's action in creatures (which, of course, is only an aspect of divine Being), is a *creating* action. Far from taking from the reality of the creature's own action it actually provides the creature with an action which is its very own. Once again God's action in creatures is the presence in creatures of *Being*.

In order, then, to be present in creatures and active in them, God does not have to take away anything to make room for the divine presence and the divine activity; on the contrary, it is this very divine presence and action which gives the creature everything. As Piet Schoonenberg puts it:

> God ... does not take over the work of a worldly cause, he supersedes nothing, he eliminates nothing (*The Christ*, p 25-6).

> The creator ... realises all being and activity in the world as a being and activity of the worldly beings themselves (p 19).

To help us to see how God's action does not cancel out the action of creatures, but, being of a different order from theirs, works to make their own action possible, Schoonenberg gives what he calls 'a weak simile':

I can by virtue of my own free will move my arm, but in doing so my personal freedom in no way takes the place of the biochemical reactions which cause this movement. My person does not stand aside from those organic factors, cannot be added to them, replaces none of them. This is a weak simile for God's rule in the world (*The Christ*, p 25).

Creator and creatures are not rivals. This, interestingly, is true even when a free creature sets himself or herself in opposition to God: for, paradoxically, this free act too is given by God (here that problem of evil arises again). To see God's involvement in creation or in the Bible, or, what concerns us in the present context, in Jesus – even in Jesus' freedom – as taking away from the action or involvement or freedom of creatures themselves, is, then, to make a very serious mistake indeed. It is to put God's action and that of creatures on the same level. Consequently, it is to put the Creator on the same level as creatures. It is to forget altogether that creatures have their own being only because and in so far as they participate in Being. It is to set up an entirely false dilemma. Instead of it being a case of 'either God or creature', the truth is, in fact, quite the opposite: the truth is that 'without God, nothing creaturely at all – no creaturely being, no creaturely action'.

'Two natures'

The radical difference between Creator and creature or, in this case, between the Creator and the human creature, is a point which, it seems to me, is generally overlooked when people think about Jesus. It is not taken into account, or at least is not sufficiently brought into the open, when, for example, it is said that Jesus had 'two natures', a human 'nature' and a divine 'nature'. This, as those familiar with the language of the catechism will know, is a commonly used statement, and one which would be regarded as very correct theologically and as very acceptable. Already in Chapter Eight I have referred to the problem attached to the use today of the word 'nature' in this context and how it can suggest that the human reality in Jesus was a static inert 'block'. It seems to me that the use here of the word 'two' is also bound to create problems. For if we reflect on it, we will realise, I think, that 'two' is a word which we use only (or at least normally) when there is question of referring to, not just one reality, but also another of the same kind: thus we can talk about two people or two animals or two creatures. God, however, as we ought to realise, is not a second reality of the same kind as *any* other: after all, the most radical difference of all is the difference between God and everything else. To refer, then, to the coming together of the divine and human in Jesus as the coming together of 'two natures' or, indeed of 'two' of anything, seems to me to suggest that in Jesus there is a coming together of two realities of the same kind. Inevitably this leads to confused thinking and gives rise to all kinds of problems. It gives rise, for example, to the problem of trying to see how it is that one of the 'natures' does not have to make room for itself, and so to take room from the other, in order to be present with the other.

This difference between the divine and human is, interestingly, something of which we seem to be very aware in certain contexts. When, for example, we are talking about a room in which there is one person present, we would never say that really there are 'two' there, even though we believe that God is actually 'present' there also. Nor would it ever occur to us to say that God's 'presence' there means that there is, then, less room available for creatures! In contexts like these we show clearly that we know that God's 'presence' is of such a radically different kind from that of a creature that there can be no conflict, no 'either … or' dilemma. In the context of the coming together of the divine and human in Jesus, however, we seem to forget this radical difference.

To avoid giving the wrong impression and, so, becoming confused or causing confusion, we need to find a way of talking about the coming together of the divine and human in Jesus which would bring out the fact that there is a coming together here, not of two beings, but of Being and a being. An image which I myself find helpful, along with that of Piet Schoonenberg given above, is one suggested by the American theologian, Frederick E. Crowe:

> I suggest the image of a heaven filled with pure light, which gives reality to the colour of the earthly world without depriving it of its proper character and certainly not lying beside it like block beside block. In some such way the divine being joins human nature in Christ to become the one God-man (*God, Jesus, and Spirit*, ed. Daniel Callahan, p 110).

* * *

The argument stated at the beginning of this chapter might seem a very plausible one indeed. It might seem very convincing to say that the more the human being, Jesus of Nazareth, belonged to God, the less he necessarily belonged to himself and that the more his human freedom belonged to God as God's very own, the less free Jesus himself was. This argument can, however, be expressed in other terms. It can be stated thus: the more Jesus' created being was rooted and immersed in Being, the less being of his own Jesus possessed; the more Jesus' created free being was rooted and immersed in Free Being, the less of free being it had. Put this way, we can see that the argument is not at all as plausible as it might seem. In fact, we can see that the opposite is, in fact, the case. Jesus had his created being, his own created being, precisely because and in so far as this was rooted and immersed in Being; Jesus had his created *free* being, his own created free being, precisely because and in so far as this was rooted and immersed in Being, the Source of all freedom. God and creatures, Being and the beings, are not rivals. As Karl Rahner puts it:

> ... closeness to God and active independence of a creature grow in direct, not in inverse proportion ... that means the freedom of the creature ... is perfected by being totally given over to God (*Sacramentum Mundi*, vol 3, p 206).

Paradoxical, then, as it may seem, far from being less free, less 'his own person', by the fact that he was so given over to God, Jesus was *more* independent and free precisely because he was so given over to God:

> Thus Christ is most radically man, and his humanity is the freest and most independent, not in spite of, but because of its being taken up, by being constituted as the self-utterance of God ... Since *God* 'goes out' of himself, this form of his existence has the most radical validity, force and reality (Karl Rahner, *Theological Investigations*, vol 4, p 117).

What is true of Jesus is, of course, true of all of us: we really *are* in so far as we are *grounded*.

CHAPTER TWELVE

Could we have Jesus, but without 'God'?

The particular aspect of the relationship between Jesus and God with which this book has been primarily concerned is *what* Christians believe about this. Another question can also be asked: *Why* do Christians associate the word 'God' with Jesus at all? Why not speak of him simply as a good human being, even as the perfect human being and leave it at that?

This, of course, touches on the most fundamental of all religious questions: Why believe in 'God'? It is a topic which, if it were to be dealt with in any adequate way, would require a book in its own right. The most that can be done here is to suggest an approach to the matter – mainly with a view to pointing the way to further study.

In order to see why the word 'God' should be associated with Jesus, obviously it is necessary to reflect on why anyone should ever use that word 'God' at all. It is necessary, in other words, to understand the *religious* perception of life because it is only when we have this perception that we can speak with conviction of 'God'. To have such a sense, or even to understand it, we need, I suggest, to be aware of the world as 'symbolic'.

Symbol

Part of our everyday experience is that at least certain things can have a depth of meaning and that there is more to them than immediately meets the eye. It is to this aspect of life, this multi-layered dimension of reality, that the word 'symbol' refers. The following sentence from Roger Hazelton describes symbol well:

There is more than appears on the surface, and yet the surface is where the depth begins to appear (*Ascending Flame, Descending Dove*, p 44).

Since symbol is a feature of our everyday experience, examples abound. One obvious example is the spoken word. There is more to this than the sound which 'appears' on the surface. Anyone who can hear at all, even a baby, can experience the sound itself. But only those who are able not just to hear but to understand, can get beneath the surface and can experience the meaning contained in it. Take away the sound, however, and the meaning ceases to be conveyed – 'the surface is where the depth begins to appear'. Another everyday example is the human body. There is more to this than appears on the surface: there is the person embodied there. But it is only in and through the body that the person 'begins to appear'. A warm handshake, seen superficially, would appear to be two people just squeezing hands. But anyone who sees beneath the surface of what is happening here will see that this physical contact is embodying, expressing and conveying such deep human feelings as sympathy or support or shared joy.

Symbol is often dismissed as 'merely a sign'. A symbol is, indeed, a sign in that it always points to something beyond itself. But it is not 'a *mere* sign' if by that phrase is meant that a symbol only points to something outside itself, as a signpost points to the next town. A symbol actually embodies and makes present the reality to which it points: a body gives presence to the person; a word embodies the thoughts of the speaker; the warm handshake conveys the deepest of human feelings.

The religious perception of reality

Awareness of the symbolic nature of the world will not automatically give us a basis for religious belief. Without it, however, we will find it rather difficult to see why the word 'God' has to be part of our vocabulary and, more particularly in the present context, why Christians associate it with Jesus.

To have a basis for religious belief, we need to perceive the presence in life of what is called 'the divine'. The steps necessary for such a perception are difficult ones. *How* deep, we need to ask, is the depth which only begins to appear on the surface? How *much* more is there to the world and to life than appears on its surface? Is the 'more' just a little more or even just a lot more? The peculiar insight which is the basis of religious belief is, in general terms at least, that there are in life hints of what is literally immeasurably more than appears on the surface, echoes of depths appearing there which are literally unfathomable. Religious belief is aware of the puzzling nature of life – its tragedy and its comedy, its joys and its pains, its hopes and its fears, its successes and its failures, its love and its hate, its beauty and its ugliness, people's capacity for good and evil, their ability to think both the most noble and the most ignoble thoughts. But it perceives that

> … in all our thoughts and language there is a resonance of the infinite, as its deepest background (*A New Catechism*, p 17).

It perceives, for example, that every experience which we have, whether it be of love or of beauty or even of loneliness and pain, is suggestive of even further possibilities. We may say of a beautiful sunset or flower or person: 'This is the last word, the ultimate in beauty'. But we never really mean that it is: we know, deep down at least, that even this is only the surface beneath which there are depths which still do not appear and, furthermore, that these depths too invite probing – a thought which Tennyson expresses:

> … all experience is an arch wherethrough
> Gleams that untravelled world whose margin fades
> For ever and for ever when I move (*Ulysses*).

Religious belief is basically a conviction that there are, in our experience of life, hints of a 'Beyond' Reality which, to use Rudolf Otto's language, is both awesome and alluring (*tremendum et fascinans*). It is 'awesome', in that in its presence we feel that the ground on which we are standing is, indeed, 'holy' (*cf* Ex 3:5). It is 'alluring' in that it is not just distantly 'there', but is involved with us and is involving us with 'Itself'. Religious belief is an awareness of *Being*, of which the world of our experience is an expression and a reflection, as engaging us and as evoking wonder and worship. It is an awareness which Wordsworth seems to have had in an unusually intense way above *Tintern Abbey*:

> ... And I have felt
> A presence that disturbs me with the joy
> Of elevated thoughts, a sense sublime
> Of something far more deeply interfused,
> Whose dwelling is the light of setting suns,
> And the round ocean and the living air,
> And the blue sky, and in the mind of man:
> A motion and a spirit, that impels
> All thinking things, all objects of all thought ...

The religious insight, though available to all, does not come automatically or always easily. Certainly it cannot be arrived at just by learning doctrine by rote – no more than can the insight into the deeper meaning and beauty of music or art or poetry be arrived at simply in that way. *Reflection* is necessary – reflection on, for example, the superabundance of which the beauty of a person or a thing is suggestive; or on the boundless ocean onto which we launch when we begin to think of that with which the human spirit can be concerned. *Listening* is necessary – listening, for example, to those deep sounds which can really be heard only in silence. *Doing* is necessary – responding, for example, to the cry of the poor ones in our world, and becoming aware at least of the endless road along which answering this cry could lead us.

In trying to enter into, or to understand, the religious perception of life, it can be helpful to recall that throughout history certain experiences have been found to disclose this Presence in a particularly striking way. Always evocative was, for example, the awesomeness of the mountain, be it Horeb or Sinai or Tabor or Croagh Patrick. Suggestive too was the life-giving freshness of water, be it the ocean or the common well-spring or the great river, for example, the Ganges or the Jordan or 'the waters of Babylon'. The vastness, the loneliness and the barrenness of the wilderness brought biblical figures in particular into contact with the silence of their being and with the distant sounds which could be heard echoed there. *More* – much more, than appears on the surface – was perceived in the life-force experienced in the springtime. *Superabundance* seemed pointed to in the fruitfulness and harvest of autumn. To draw attention to that *More* and to celebrate that *Superabundance*, these places and seasons were celebrated in ritual – in rites, for example, of spring and mid-summer and mid-winter, all of which pre-date our Christian feasts. Birth, marriage and death always evoked a sense of awe which cried out to be celebrated in ritual, so that these events have always, everywhere, been surrounded by ritual. In a world, then, which was experienced as symbolic of the presence of the 'Beyond' or the 'Divine', certain seasons and events and places were, and still can be, perceived as focusing in an unusually intense way this Presence and this Power which believers call 'God'.

Jesus: Symbol of God

Christians link Jesus with God in the close way in which they do because, briefly, they believe that in him, above all, the *More*, with all its strangeness, appears in a unique way: it appears in a unique way, they believe, in all the events surrounding the life and death and destiny of this man – in what he said and did, in the way he lived and died, in his teaching and his loving, his touching and his healing, his vision for our world and his commitment to that vision and, above all, in the experience of his being brought through death. Jesus, of all people, is, in the Christian experience, the one in whom 'there is more than appears on the surface, and yet the surface is where the depths begins to appear'. He, of all people, is the symbol and embodiment of that *mysterium tremendum et fascinans* of which Otto speaks, that immeasurable and incalculable *More* which is both awesome and alluring, which is beyond and yet near, distant and yet beckoning. They believe that to miss this in Jesus is, when all is said, to fail to see this man in depth and, so, to stop short of really coming to terms with the truth about him. It is for this reason that, in the Christian view, we cannot understand Jesus except in terms of God.

Epilogue

Epilogue

In Brian Friel's play *Wonderful Tennessee* a small family group are waiting, on a remote pier in Donegal, for a boat to bring them out to *Oileán Draíochta*, 'Island of Otherness; Island of Mystery', as Berna translates the Irish name. The game which Angela invented to pass the time while waiting for the boat (it never actually came), was an interesting one. The idea was to pitch stones at a bottle which had been placed in position, and the aim was:

> ... to get as close as possible to that bottle. But everytime you touch it you lose a point.

As for the name of the game, Angela said:

> It's called: how close can you get without touching it (*Act Two*).

Jesus of Nazareth, being for Christians the climax of God's involvement in creation, the unmatched and unsurpassable presence of God in history, is this *Oileán Draíochta*, 'Island of Otherness; Island of Mystery'. The boat which would lead us to a full understanding of Jesus and to a clear view of the precise manner in which Christians find the mystery in him, is one for which we will always be waiting. The aim of christology, then, can only be that of Angela's game: '... how close can you get without touching it'.

This book obviously has not explained Jesus and the otherness and the mystery which Christians, over the centuries and still today, find in him. Strangely, this, like not actually hitting the bottle in Angela's game, is to the credit of any book on Jesus. Had the book even set out to do this, it would then surely have 'lost a point'. In that case, instead of penetrating the mystery, it would have missed it. In Friel's play the character Frank, wondering if the monks who had once lived on that island beyond had actually been in touch with the mystery and had, perhaps, written it all down (it could only be in 'A book without words'), says:

> And if they accomplished that, they'd have written the last book ever written – and the most wonderful! And then, Terry, then maybe life would cease! (*Act One, Scene Two*).

The group on the pier in Donegal never succeeded in reaching the misty island beyond. But, interestingly, they did experience something of the 'otherness', the 'mystery'. They experienced it where they were, as they were, in their human situation, with all its tangled messiness, on a remote, unused, stone pier 'grained with yellow and grey lichen'. They encountered it in the only place in which it can ever be encountered, either in Jesus or in ourselves – in the human.

Questions about the gospels

Modern biblical scholarship gives rise to many questions in a Christian's mind, especially regarding the gospels. What does Christian faith mean when it says that the gospels are *inspired* by God? If we are to allow that John, for example, presents Jesus as speaking during his life in a way that he did not actually speak, in what sense can Christians talk about the *truth* of the gospels? And, if the intention of the gospels is not to give us a straight *Life of Jesus* but, rather, the early Church's post-resurrection faith in him, can we know any *historical facts* at all about Jesus or is it only to the disciples' faith that we have access in these documents? Questions such as these are, obviously, of major importance to Christians and are, as one would expect, ones with which scholars of the Bible deal and with which the 1964 *Instruction* encourages them to deal. As has been said in Chapter Three, only a few points in this regard can be made here. In pursuing such questions the interested reader should find the references given in the notes to Chapter Two and Chapter Three helpful. A very accessible treatment of the gospels is Peter Schmidt's *How to Read the Gospels: Historicity and truth in the Gospels and Acts*, translated by C. Vanhove-Romanik (Maynooth, Ireland, St Pauls, 1993).

'Inspired'

With regard to the gospels being 'inspired' by God, as has been pointed out in Chapter Eleven, according to the Christian understanding, God's involvement in the composition of the Bible did not in any way override the activity of the human authors. The human authors are, the Council insists, 'true authors':

... while employed by God they made use of their own powers and abilities ... (*Dei Verbum*, art 11).

Just as God's involvement and presence in Jesus did not at all prevent him from being one hundred per cent a human being, so, God's involvement in the writing of the Bible did not at all prevent the human authors from being one hundred per cent the authors of their respective books; just as the only way in which we might find God in Jesus is by taking him seriously as a human being, so the only way in which we might find God's Word in the gospels is by taking these seriously as human books. To recall Vatican II:

... God speaks in sacred scripture through men *in human fashion* ... (*Dei Verbum*, art. 12, emphasis mine).

Taking the gospels seriously as human documents, which is what modern biblical scholarship and the 1964 *Instruction* are doing, does not, then, in any sense run counter to belief in the divine 'inspiration' of the gospels. On the contrary, it is only being consistent with, and faithful to, that belief.

'Gospel-truth'?

With regard to the Christian conviction concerning the truth of the gospels, here the reader can be reminded, if only briefly, of what exactly this conviction is. Regarding any statement – whether it be made by the author of one of the gospels, or by G. K. Chesterton, or by a person who says that she saw the sun 'go down' last evening – we never judge its truth or falsehood by taking the words at their face value: we always judge this truth by taking into account what the author intended to say by means of the words used. What Christians believe to be free from error in the gospels – what they believe to be 'gospel-truth' – is, accordingly, what these human authors *intended to teach* about Jesus and his meaning for salvation. So, going behind the words, and trying to find out what the sacred authors meant by the words, is far from being an exercise in questioning or undermining the truth of the gospels. It is, in fact, a search for that very truth – as, again, Vatican II reminds us:

... the interpreter of sacred scripture, in order to see clearly what God wanted to communicate to us, should carefully investigate what meaning the sacred writers really intended ... for truth is expressed in a variety of ways ... (*Dei Verbum*, art 12).

The 1964 *Instruction* is even more explicit:

Unless the exegete, then, pays attention to all those factors which have a bearing on the origin and the composition of the gospels, and makes due use of the acceptable findings of modern research, he will fail in his duty of ascertaining what the intentions of the sacred writers were, and what it is that they have actually said ... (no. 2).

The Jesus of history?

As to the third matter raised, whether we can be sure of any historical facts about Jesus, the very short answer to this question is, of course, that we can: for, without facts there would be no foundation for belief at all. The faith-understanding of Jesus which we have in the gospels is, we must remember, a faith-understanding of *the Jesus who lived in history*. Basic to the gospel accounts of Jesus are, then, the words and deeds of Jesus. So, as C. H. Dodd puts it, in the gospels and in the tradition which preceded them,

... faith acted as a preservative of genuinely historical memories without which it could never have arisen (*The Founder of Christianity*, p 33).

Here it is interesting to recall, in passing, the description of Jesus which Peter gives in a speech attributed to him in the Acts of the Apostles – a speech which, as I have pointed out already, represents the earliest, pre-gospel, preaching. Addressing people who actually knew and remembered Jesus, Peter reminds them that he was

... a man commended to you by God by the miracles and portents and signs that God worked through him when he was among you, as you all know (Acts 1:22).

A Question related to the Virginal Conception

Though the virginal conception of Jesus gives rise to very many interesting and important questions – questions regarding scripture, such as the nature and meaning of the infancy narratives, questions regarding the history of doctrine, such as that of the origin and history of this particular belief, and theological questions such as the place which this belief has in the Christian scheme of things – the only question which needs to be discussed in this book has to do with Jesus being really human. How, it is often reasonably asked, can we speak of Jesus being a real, 'normal' human being if he did not have a human father? In terms of genetics, where, for example, are we to think of Jesus' chromosomes coming from?

It is very interesting to note that these are questions which scripture makes no attempt at all to answer. The infancy stories of Matthew and Luke, in which alone, as has been said, there is reference in scripture to the virginal conception, show no interest at all in the biological details, but only in the fact of the divine initiative: they simply tell the story of Jesus' conception without showing any interest at all either in explaining how, in biological terms, God might have brought this conception about, or how Jesus, nonetheless was a 'descendant of Adam'. It is interesting also that the official teaching of the Church adopts the same attitude: it also simply states that Jesus was, in the words of the creed, 'conceived of the Holy Spirit and born of the virgin Mary' without at all attempting to show how Jesus was, nonetheless, as the Council of Chalcedon defined,

... complete in humanity ... true man, ...consisting of a
rational soul and a body ... of one substance with us in
humanity, 'like us in all things apart from sin' ....

Indeed I find that theology itself is of little help in this matter.
Theologians who insist that Jesus was actually conceived of
a virgin also, obviously, insist that he was truly and really
human. Rarely, however, if ever, do we find them making
any attempt to help us to understand how these two truths
are to be reconciled. In this connection, four points – and
these only of a rather general nature – might be made here.

The first has to do with the need for a degree of openness of
mind and imagination in regard to Jesus. Interest in Jesus of
Nazareth arises in the first place because of the Christian
conviction regarding the uniqueness of this man. It arises ultimately because Christians believe that, in encountering
Jesus, they encounter in a unique way the 'God of Surprises',
to use Gerald W. Hughes' phrase. A Christian cannot, then,
expect to meet in Jesus only the ordinary but must be open
to experiencing in him new divine creative possibilities: a
Christian is, after all, one who encounters in Jesus the ultimate surprise of his being raised from the dead. A Christian
ought, then, to avoid setting limits, in a hasty and arbitrary
way, to the creative possibilities of the Creator, especially in
Jesus of Nazareth.

The second point has to do with the need to see this Church
teaching – as, indeed, every Church teaching – in perspective. Here it is useful to refer to what Vatican II describes as
'an order or "hierarchy" of truths'. To understand the concept we need to take into account certain considerations.

We need to appreciate firstly that if something is true, then,
of course, it is true and, furthermore, that if it is what Vatican II calls 'a Christian truth', then it has relevance for
Christian understanding and living: since 'a Christian truth'
is one which was made known, in some way, by God in connection with the event of Jesus, then, obviously, it must

have relevance for our lives; otherwise it would be impossible to understand why God would have made it known at all. We need to appreciate secondly that even though all the truths of faith are important and significant, not all of are *equally* important and significant. A simple example will make this clear. The truth that God has taken a new initiative in the life of Jesus of Nazareth and is involved in a unique way in the events surrounding this life, is, obviously, much more significant for a Christian than the truth that there are seven and only seven sacraments – even though this latter is something which was declared in the most solemn and official way to be true (that is, was 'defined') by the Council of Trent and was, therefore, considered by that Council to be important.

It is to these facts that Vatican II refers when it says, in its *Decree on Ecumenism*, that

> … in Catholic teaching there exists an order or 'hierarchy' of truths, since they vary in their relation to the foundation of Christian faith (art 11).

This is a matter which, the Council says, has to be kept in mind by Catholic theologians 'when comparing doctrines' (as above).

The 'hierarchy' of truths' has to be kept in mind in the present context. With regard to Jesus being actually conceived virginally, official Church teaching, while emphatically teaching this, never presents it as being, in Vatican II's words, 'the foundation of Christian faith'. As Gerald O'Collins points out:

> In the hierarchy of Christian truths the virginal conception does not rate 'at the top'. *On any showing* the personal identity and mission of Jesus as Son of God and Saviour of the world are more important than how he was conceived and the fact that he had no human father (*Interpreting Jesus*, p 196, italics mine).

The fact of Jesus being a real human being, however, does

rate 'at the top', or, to revert to Vatican II's metaphor, at the
bottom, for it is the very 'foundation' on which everything
else rests. If, after all, Jesus is not a real human being, then in
him God did not *really* become involved in human life and,
so, in 'him' the 'Word' did not really become 'flesh' at all.
This is not to suggest that Vatican II's notion of the 'hierarchy' of truths can be appealed to in order to justify dismiss-
ing as insignificant and irrelevant the long-standing conviction of Christians regarding the manner of Jesus' conception.
Vatican II's notion is helpful here, rather, in that it enables
us to see belief in the virginal conception of Jesus in perspective.

The third point follows from this. It is that, however we
might try to explain how Jesus can be both conceived virginally and yet be a real, 'normal' human being, there is one
way in which we may not explain it: we may not explain it
by sacrificing the human in Jesus. Whatever else we may
say, we may not say that, because Jesus was virginally conceived, he was not a *true* member of the race, not a *real* son
of 'Adam', not *one hundred per cent* a human being.

The fourth point has to do with the need to leave space,
even in the area of faith, for problems which cannot – yet at
least – be solved and for questions to which we have not yet
a clear answer – a point made by Karl Rahner in the very
context of the virginity of Mary (though not precisely in the
context of the virginal conception of Jesus). In life as a
whole we live with unresolved problems. With regard to
how we might think of Jesus as being *both* virginally conceived and *also* a real human being, we might find consoling
what Rahner says:

> Is it really necessary, after all, always to give an unambig-
> uous answer immediately to all questions which arise in
> faith and in theology? Even in the dimension of faith a
> space may be left open for what is uncertain and unan-
> swered ... (*Theological Investigations*, vol 19, pp 227-8)

The Theological Term: 'Hypostatic' Unity – A Note

As has been said in Chapter Eight, the word which theology has coined to describe the unique unity between Jesus and God is 'hypostatic'. Accordingly, the union or unity between Jesus and the Word of God is known in theology as the 'hypostatic' union or unity. The word 'hypostatic', coming as it does from the Greek *hypostasis*, echoes another age and culture. As one might expect, it is a word about which much has been written in the past and continues to be written today. It would be impossible, and indeed undesirable, to attempt to summarise in a general book of this kind the very many views of even modern theologians concerning this matter. The discussion of the word *hypostasis*, attempting as it does to express in very precise philosophical terms the relationship between Jesus and the Word, inevitably becomes very technical. It seems enough for the purposes of this book to make three rather general points regarding this word.

The first is that, in simple terms, 'hypostatic' says nothing more about the relationship between the created Word of God, Jesus, and the eternal Word of God than has been said already in the course of this book, especially in Chapter Ten. It says that Jesus was the Self-expression of the Word of God in such a way that his life and history was, in an ultimate sense, the life and history of the eternal Word of God: to refer to the image of the artist used in that chapter, it says that in an ultimate sense this divine Self-portrait did not belong to himself, but to the divine artist of whose Being he is a created extension. It says, in other words, that in Jesus of Nazareth and the eternal Word of God there is, ultimately, only one Subject, or, in Greek, one *hypostasis*, in question. To use Karl Rahner's phrase, 'the ultimate bearer' of this human life, the one who, ultimately, was 'personally' present and active and involved here, was and is the eternal Word of God. Because Jesus of Nazareth and the eternal Word of God are united in the one Subject, *hypostasis*, Jesus is said to be 'hypostatically' united to, and one with, the eternal Word of God.

The second point has to do with an English word which is commonly used to translate the Greek *hypostasis*, that is, the word 'person'. Once again this is a word about which philosophers and theologians have much to say. The point which needs to be made here is a very general, but a very important one. It is that the use of this English word 'person' in this context can give rise to serious misunderstandings today, similar, in fact, to those to which, as I have pointed out in Chapter Eight, the use of the word 'nature' can give rise. This is because of the everyday meaning which 'person' now has. In everyday English the word is now used to describe a creature who is composed of body and spirit and is intelligent and free – in other words, it is used to describe 'a human being'. Anytime we encounter a human being we can, and often do, say today: 'There is a human person'. Indeed, it is interesting to note that, outside the context of christology, the word 'person' is used in this way today even in official Church documents: so, the theologian Gerald O'Collins shows, by giving examples, that recent papal encyclicals can, as he says

> … resemble ordinary speech in its fluid and flexible uses of 'nature', 'person' and 'man' (*Interpreting Jesus*, p 182).

To say, then, as the official teaching of the Christian community does, that Jesus and the eternal Word of God share the one *hypostasis*, and to translate *hypostasis* as 'person', might very easily give a wrong impression today. It might seem to be saying that, according to the belief of the Church,

Jesus was not one of those intelligent and free creatures to whom in everyday English we refer as 'persons' but that the human 'nature' of Jesus was that inert block of humanity, altogether devoid of 'personality', to which I have referred in the course of the book. It might seem to be saying, in other words, that Jesus was not a human being at all. This – as ought to be very clear at this stage – is not what Church teaching intends to say: such a view of Jesus would be altogether heretical. As has been pointed out, that which is referred to in theology as the human 'nature' of Jesus is not, in the words of the *Concise Theological Dictionary*,

> ... a static thing, nor does it lack anything that characterizes the human 'person': presence to himself, freedom, a dialogical creaturely relationship with God through adoration and obedience ... (Karl Rahner-Herbert Vorgrimler, p. 381).

The word 'person' (*hypostasis*) as used in the context of christology obviously, then, does not have precisely the same meaning as the words 'person' and 'personality' have in the everyday speech today. 'Person', as a translation of *hypostasis*, is obviously used in a technical sense, referring generally to that ultimate centre of unity which, Christians believe, exists between this human being, Jesus of Nazareth, and the eternal Word of God.

These considerations lead to our third and closely related point. They alert us to the precise sense in which it is said that the man Jesus does not belong to himself, but rather to the Word of God. For he is not said *simply* to belong to the eternal Word of God and not to belong at all to himself. This becomes clear when we remember that Jesus stood before God as a free and (in that sense) independent human being. Being free and independent, he obviously fully belonged to himself in freedom. Being free, he was able to utter his own free *human* 'I': he was able, for example, to stand before the 'Father' and say in freedom '*I give you* thanks'. In that sense he can be said, as theologians today particularly tend to say, to be a distinct, free, *human* subject: he can be said to be, as it is sometimes put, a distinct 'psychological' subject. However, since in the Christian view this free human 'psychological' subject, Jesus of Nazareth, was a created extension of divine Being, he belonged to God as God's very own free *human subject*. So, the free *human* 'I' which Jesus uttered was, ultimately, the free *human* 'I' of the eternal Word of God: since the divine artist lived and moved in and through this Self-portrait, the eternal Word of God was always the 'One' who was the ultimate Subject in question in the life and history of Jesus. To say that the eternal Word of God was the one *hypostasis* in Jesus' case is, then, to say that the human being, Jesus, was not closed off in himself or isolated in his being – was not, as the classic definition of *hypostasis* would say, 'incommunicable to another' (*alteri incommunicabilis*) – but was, in his being, completely given over to the Word of God and, so, belonged to the *hypostasis* of the Word of God. Though he was a distinct 'psychological' subject from the eternal Word, in the order of being, however, that is, 'ontologically', he and the Word of God were one and the same subject. In that sense the Council of Ephesus says:

> One and the same is the eternal Son of the Father and the Son of the Virgin Mary, born in time after the flesh; therefore she may rightly be called Mother of God.

Concerning the formulas in which the Church tries to express who Jesus of Nazareth is – formulas which sometimes seem complicated and difficult – Aloys Grillmeier says:

> Now these formulas clarify only one, albeit the decisive, point of belief in Christ: that in Jesus Christ God really entered into human history and thus achieved our salvation. If the picture of Christ is to be illuminated fully, these formulas must always be seen against the whole background of the biblical belief in Christ ... (*Christ in Christian Tradition*, vol I, p 556).

Notes

NOTES TO CHAPTER ONE

Further Reading

Grillmeier, Aloys, *Christ in Christian Tradition*, vol. I (London: Mowbrays, second revised edition, 1975);

  'Monotheletism' in *Sacramentum Mundi*, vol 4, ed. Karl Rahner (London: Burns & Oates, 1969).

Kasper, Walter, *Jesus the Christ*, (London: Burns & Oates, 1976).

Loewe, William P, 'Chalcedon, Council of' in *The New Dictionary of Theology*, ed. J.A Komonchak, M. Collins, D. Lane (Dublin: Gill and Macmillan, 1987).

McDermott, Brian O., *Word Become Flesh: Dimensions of Christology* (Collegeville, Minnesota, A Michael Glazier Book, Liturgical Press, 1993).

Rahner, Karl, 'Current Problems in Christology' in *Theological Investigations*, vol 1 (London: Darton, Longman & Todd, 1966).

Rahner, Karl - Vorgrimler, Herbert, *Concise Theological Dictionary* (London: Burns & Oates, second edition, 1983).

Richardson, Alan, *Creeds In The Making* (London: S.C.M. Press Ltd, second edition, 1941).

Young, Frances, *The Making of the Creeds* (London: S.C.M. Press Ltd, 1991).

* * *

For an account of the christology of Apollinarius, see Aloys Grillmeier's *Christ in Christian Tradition*, vol I, pp 329-343.

The phrase about monophysitism quoted from the *Concise Theological Dictionary* is taken from p 316.

I do not introduce the christology of Arius (d 336) as it would not be helpful to do so in the present context. Here I am talking about the tendency throughout history to sacrifice the human in Jesus so as to make place for the divine. Though Arius and his followers also held that Jesus was not truly human, they did not really adopt this position so as to make place for the divine in Jesus: Arius believed that the Word is not really divine, but creaturely. For an account of Arianism see Alan Richardson, *op cit*, pp 52ff, Frances Young, *op cit*, pp 43f, Aloys Grillmeier, *op cit*, Chapter Two, especially pp 238f.

In the early centuries the tendency to understand Jesus as one who was first of all 'divine' (and sometimes to sacrifice the human in him) was associated particularly with the Alexandrian school of theology. The opposite approach, that of starting with the human being, Jesus (and sometimes failing to do justice to the divine) was associated particularly with the theology of the school at Antioch. The controversies of these early centuries were, then, to a large extent controversies between these two schools. See, for example, Richardson (*op cit*) pp 71f, and Young (*op cit*), chapters 3 and 5.

For a brief accounts of monothelitism see Aloys Grillmeier *art cit*, *loc cit*, also Karl Rahner-Herbert Vorgrimler, article 'Monothelitism', *loc cit*.

For brief accounts of the Council of Chalcedon and the events leading up to it, see Richardson, *op cit*, pp 81ff, Young, *op cit*, chapter 5, and William P. Loewe *art cit*, Aloys Grillmeier, *op cit*, pp 488f.

NOTES TO CHAPTER TWO

Further Reading:

Brown, Raymond E., *The Birth of the Messiah* (New York: Doubleday, 1979; 'Aspects of New Testament Thought: Christology' in *The New Jerome Biblical Commentary*, ed R.E. Brown and others, (London: Chapman, 1990);
   Responses to 101 Questions on the Bible (New York: Paulist Press, 1990);
   An Adult Christ at Christmas (Collegeville: The Liturgical Press, 1978);
   A Coming Christ in Advent (Collegeville: The Liturgical Press, 1988).

Dodd, C.H., *The Founder of Christianity* (London: Collins, 1971).

Fitzmyer, Joseph A., *A Christological Catechism* (New York: Paulist Press, 1991).

Harrington, Wilfrid, *The Drama of Christ's Coming* (Dublin: Dominican Publications, 1988);
   The Jesus Story (Dublin: Columba Press, 1991).

Neirynck, Frans, 'Synoptic Problem' in *The New Jerome Biblical Commentary*, ed R.E. Brown and others (London: Geoffrey Chapman, 1990).

Schillebeeckx, Edward, *Jesus: An Experiment in Christology* (London: Collins, 1979).

***

The Chesterton reference in the text is to the first verse of his poem *The Donkey*, see *G.K Chesterton, Stories, Essays, and Poems* (London: J. M. Dent & Sons Ltd., 1935), p 283.

For the text of the 1964 *Instruction* and commentary, see Joseph A. Fitzmyer, *op cit*, pp 119f.

The order in which the gospels were written is discussed by Frans Neirynck *art cit*, *loc cit*, 587-595.

For Brown's division of the first century into thirds, see *Responses*, pp 55ff.

For the development of early christology, see R.E. Brown, *The Birth of the Messiah*, pp 29-32; *An Adult Christ at Christmas*, pp 1-19; 'Aspects of New Testament Thought: Christology', *loc cit*, pp 1357f (81:12-19); Joseph A. Fitzmyer, *op cit*, pp 24f; Wilfrid Harrington, *The Drama of Christ's Coming*, pp 12-14; *The Jesus Story*, Chapter 1; Edward Schillebeeckx, *op cit*, pp 550f. (There is evidence that at an even earlier stage in the Christian understanding of Jesus the 'second coming' of Christ, the *parousia*, was thought of as 'the christological moment' – see Raymond E. Brown, 'Aspects of New Testament Thought: Christology', *loc cit*, p 1357: 81: 13; also *The Birth of the Messiah*, p 29, note 14).

The phrase 'the christological moment' is explained by Raymond E. Brown in 'Aspects of New Testament Thought: Christology', *loc cit*, p 1537 (81:12). It does not refer to a moment in which Jesus himself actually became Son, Lord, Christ, etc. It refers rather to a moment in which the disciples recognised a reality which was already there.

Harrington's 'casting back' phrase is used in *The Drama of Christ's Coming*, p 13.

On Rom 1: 4, see Brown, *An Adult Christ at Christmas*, p 7, Harrington, *The Drama of Christ's Coming*, p 12.

Brown uses the phrase 'the chronologically backwards-growth' in the early understanding of Christ in *An Adult Christ At Christmas*, p 6, and speaks of 'a backwards process' of the development of Christology in *The Birth of the Messiah*, p 32.

Brown speaks of 'second-generation Christians' in *Responses*, p 57.

Regarding the writings about Jesus which existed before the gospels, see Fitzmyer, *op cit*, pp 9, 25, and Frans Neirynck, *art cit, loc cit*, pp 587f (40).

NOTES TO CHAPTER THREE

Further reading:
See notes to chapter two, and also the following:
Bausch, William J., *Storytelling: Imagination and Faith*, (Mystic: Twenty-Third Publications, 1984).
Brown, Raymond E., *A Crucified Christ in Holy Week: Essays on the Four Gospel Passion Narratives* (Collegeville: The Liturgical Press, 1986); *The Gospel and Epistles of John, A Concise Commentary* (Collegeville: The Liturgical Press, 1988).
Crossan, John D., *The Dark Interval: Towards a Theology of Story*, (Miles, Illinois, Argus Communications, 1975).
McDermott, Brian O.,*Word Become Flesh: Dimensions of Christology* (Col-

legeville, Minnesota: A Michael Glazier Book, The Liturgical Press, 1993).

Schmidt, Peter, *How to Read the Gospels: Historicity and truth in the Gospels and Acts*, trans C. Vanhove-Romanik, (Maynooth, Ireland, St Pauls, 1993).

Shea, John, *Stories of Faith*, (Chicago: The Thomas More Press, 1980).

Shaw, Bernard, *St Joan* (Harmondsworth, Middlesex: Penguin Books, 1948).

***

Regarding the identity of the four evangelists, see R. E. Brown, *Responses*, p 59; *The Gospel and Epistles of John, A Concise Commentary*, pp 9f; J. A. Fitzmyer, *op cit*, p 25; W. Harrington, *The Jesus Story*, pp 14f.

For a brief and accessible but scholarly treatment of the four accounts of the Passion, see R.E. Brown, *A Crucified Christ in Holy Week: Essays on the Four Gospel Passion Narratives* .

Raymond E. Brown describes the Jesus of John as 'omniscient' and 'emphatically knowing' in *A Crucified Christ in Holy Week*, p 57 (see also note 19). Of 'the Jesus who comes at last to his hour in the Fourth Gospel' he says:

> He is a Jesus conscious of his pre-existence. Through death, therefore, he is returning to a state he has temporarily left during his stay in this world (17:5). He is not a victim at the mercy of his opponents since he has freely chosen to lay down his life with the utter certitude that he will take it up again (10:17-18). If there is an element of struggle in the passion, it is a struggle without suspense, for the Satanic prince of this world has no power over Jesus (14:30). Since the Johannine Jesus is omniscient (2:25; 6:6; etc.), he cannot be caught off guard by what will happen in the passion. He had chosen Judas knowing that Judas was going to betray him (6:70-71) and has himself sent Judas off on his evil mission (13:27-30) – *ibid.*

Brown makes the point about John's picture of Jesus being the dominant one in Christian piety *ibid*, note 19.

The quotation from Brian Friel is taken from *Wonderful Tennessee* (Oldcastle, Ireland: The Gallery Press, 1993), p 61.

NOTES TO CHAPTER FOUR

Further reading:

Fitzmyer, Joseph A., *A Christological Catechism* (New York: Paulist Press, 1991).

Harrington, Daniel J., 'The Gospel According to Mark' in *The New Jerome Biblical Commentary*, ed R. E. Brown and others (London: Geoffrey Chapman, 1990).

Karris, Robert J., 'The Gospel According to Luke' in *The New Jerome Biblical Commentary*, ed R. E. Brown and others (London: Geoffrey Chapman, 1990).

Macquarrie, John, *Principles of Christian Theology* (London: SCM Press, revised edition, 1977).

McDermott, Brian O., *Word Become Flesh: Dimensions of Christology* , (Collegeville, Minnesota: A Michael Glazier Book, Liturgical Press, 1993).

O'Collins, Gerald, *Interpreting Jesus* (London, Chapman, 1983).

Rahner, Karl, *Foundations of Christian Faith* (London: Darton, Longman & Todd, 1978), VI;
    'Current Problems in Christology' in *Theological Investigations*, vol 1, (London: Darton, Longman & Todd, 1961);
    'Incarnation' and 'Jesus Christ' in *Sacramentum Mundi*, vol 3, ed. Karl Rahner, (London: Burns & Oates, 1969).

Schoonenberg, Piet, *The Christ*, (New York: Herder and Herder, 1971).

Viviano, Benedict T., 'The Gospel According to Matthew' in *The New Jerome Biblical Commentary*, ed R. E. Brown and others (London: Geoffrey Chapman, 1990).

***

The question as to whether or not Jesus was a creature arose in the Arian controversy in the fourth century. But the context in which it then arose was different from the present one. The question in that controversy concerned whether the 'Word' who 'was made flesh' in Jesus was God or a creature. Arius, as is well known, said the 'Word' is not really God but a creature, a position which was, of course, rejected by the Council of Nicea in 325. In our present context the question is not whether the 'Word' is a creature – in the words of the prologue of the gospel according to John, '... the Word was God' – but, rather, whether Jesus, the one in whom the divine 'Word' became flesh, faced God with a sense of creatureliness. How Jesus, the carpenter from Nazareth, was related to the eternal 'Word' who was God will be discussed in Section Four of this book. But before we can say in what sense this human being, Jesus of Nazareth, was the eternal 'Word' incarnate, we need first to ensure that the one about whom we are speaking is a human being who, therefore, stood before God with a sense of creatureliness.

On the subject of Jesus' freedom and sinlessness (his *de facto* sinlessness and how we might think of him being incapable of sinning) see Gerald O' Collins, *op cit*, pp 193f; Brian O. McDermott, *op cit*, pp 205f; Piet Schoonenberg, *op cit*, pp. 135f; John Macquarrie, *op cit*, pp 301f; Karl Rahner, 'Current Problems in Christology', *loc cit*, pp 160-161, n 2).

For a brief treatment of the gospels' accounts of the temptations of Jesus
see Joseph A. Fitzmyer, *op cit*, pp 44-5; Daniel J. Harrington, *art cit, loc cit*,
p 597 (41: 6); Benedict T. Viviano, *art cit, loc cit*, p 638 (42: 19); Robert J Karris, *art cit, loc cit*, pp 688-689 (43: 52-54).

NOTES TO CHAPTER FIVE

Further reading:

Brown, Raymond E., *Jesus God and Man* (London: Geoffrey Chapman,
1968);

The Birth of the Messiah (New York: Doubleday, An Image Book, 1979).

Fitzmyer, Joseph A., *A Christological Catechism* (New York: Paulist Press,
1991).

Gutwenger, Englebert, 'The Problem of Christ's Knowledge' in *Concilium*,
vol 1, no 2, Jan 1966.

Jung, Carl G., *Memories, Dreams, Reflections*, Recorded and Edited by
Aniela Jaffe (New York: Vintage Books, 1989).

Macquarrie, John, *Principles of Christian Theology*, (London: S.C.M. Press,
revised edition, 1977).

McDermott, Brian O., *Word Become Flesh: Dimensions of Christology*, (Collegeville, Minnesota: A Michael Glazier Book, Liturgical Press, 1993).

O'Collins, Gerald, *Interpreting Jesus* (London: Chapman, 1983).

Rahner, Karl, 'Dogmatic Reflections on The Knowledge and Self-
Consciousness of Christ', in *Theological Investigations*, vol 5 (London:
Darton, Longman & Todd, 1966);

'Incarnation' and 'Jesus Christ' in *Sacramentum Mundi*, vol 3, ed. Karl
Rahner, (London: Burns & Oates, 1969);

'Reflection on the Concept of 'Ius Divinum' in Catholic Thought' in
Theological Investigations, vol 5 (London: Darton, Longman & Todd,
1966);

Foundations of Christian Faith (London: Darton, Longman & Todd, 1978).

Schoonenberg, Piet, *The Christ* (New York: Herder and Herder, 1971).

* * *

For the connection between the being of Jesus and his consciousness, see
Karl Rahner, *Theological Investigations*, vol 1, pp. 168ff and vol 5, pp 193ff.
Rahner, starting from 'the axiom of the thomistic metaphysics of knowledge according to which being, and self-awareness, are elements of the
one reality which condition each other immanently', holds that '... a
purely ontic *Unio hypostatica* is metaphysically impossible to conceive'
(vol 5, pp 205-6).

Regarding Jesus' awareness of his unique role in God's plan, see also Karl
Rahner, *Sacramentum Mundi*, vol. 3, pp 115 and 204; Gerald O'Collins, *op
cit*, pp 186ff; Raymond E. Brown, *Jesus God and Man*, p. 59.

The scripture scholar, Joseph A. Fitzmyer, writing about the themes in the gospels which represent the teachings of Jesus himself, says:

> He (Jesus) acted as an agent of Yahweh, as one who could forgive sins and could interpret God's word in scripture ... An aspect of his mission can be seen in his willingness to differ with the legal attitudes of old and some widespread beliefs and customs rooted in the Old Testament itself (e.g. his attitude toward adultery (Mt 5:27) and divorce (Mk 10:2-12; Lk 16:18) ... the impact that his teaching, his ministry, and his personality made on those who heard him caused many of them to realize that he was presenting himself as someone other than the rest of mankind, and especially other than the rest of contemporary teachers and prophets of old (*A Christological Catechism*, p. 47).

For an example of how the manuals of theology tried to reconcile how Jesus could have access to unlimited knowledge and yet grow in knowledge, see G. Van Noort, *De Deo Redemptore* (Bussum in Hollandia: Paulus Brand, 1925), pp 76-77 par 113.

See Raymond E. Brown's *The Birth of the Messiah*, pp 471ff for a commentary on the boy Jesus in the Temple.

About Jesus having faith, see O'Collins, *op cit*, pp 190ff; McDermott, *op cit*, 208ff.

The concepts 'divine law' and 'divine institution' are dealt with by Karl Rahner in *Theological Investigations*, vol 5, *The Church and the Sacraments*, pp 41ff; see also *Foundations of Christian Faith*, pp 326ff.

For a very accessible account of the knowledge of Jesus in scripture, see Raymond E. Brown, *Jesus God and Man*, chapter two, also Joseph A. Fitzmyer, *A Christological Catechism*, especially, pp 86-101.

Regarding Jesus's threefold prediction of the details of his passion and death (Mk 8:31; 9:31: 10:33-34, and parallel passages), Joseph A. Fitzmyer says:

> Such passages suggest that Jesus did know what fate was in store for him. Yet when such passages are analyzed, these so-called predictions are seen to have been formulated with hindsight and include details drawn from the synoptic passion narratives. They cannot be simplistically regarded as actual predictions uttered by Jesus of Nazareth during his ministry. Yet there is no reason to question the substantial conviction that he undoubtedly had that he would die violently at the hands of his opponents. Though the classic threefold announcements prove to be stylistically formulated, they do not preclude that Jesus spoke to his disciples in a guarded fashion about a fate that might be

his in Jerusalem. Whether he had any clear knowledge of the form of that fate (e.g. by stoning, or by crucifixion) is impossible to say, and is, in fact, unlikely (*A Christological Catechism*, pp 101-2).

For an existentialist description of human existence, see John Macquarrie, *Principles of Christian Theology*, Chapter 3.

With regard to the gospels being a source for the knowledge of Jesus, Joseph A. Fitzmyer says:

Being composed at least a generation after his death, the canonical gospels cannot be regarded as first-hand evidence of his consciousness ... (*A Christological Catechism*, p 15).

NOTES TO CHAPTER SIX

Further reading:

McDermott, Brian O., *Word Become Flesh: Dimensions of Christology*, (Collegville, Minnesota: A Michael Glazier Book, 1993).

Rahner, Karl, 'Dogmatic Reflections on the Knowledge and Self-Consciousness of Christ' in *Theological Investigations*, vol. 5 (London: Darton, Longman & Todd, 1966);

'History of the World and Salvation History', *loc cit*.

'The Need for `A Short Formula' of Christian Faith' in *Theological Investigations*, vol 9 (London: Darton, Longman & Todd, 1972);

'On the Theology of the Incarnation' in *Theological Investigations*, vol 4 (London: Darton, Longman & Todd, 1966);

Foundations of Christian Faith (London: Darton, Longman & Todd, 1978).

Schillebeeckx, Edward, 'Faith Functioning in Human Self-Understanding' in *The Word in History: The St Saviour Symposium*, ed T. Patrick Burke (London: Collins, 1968);

God and Man (London and Sydney: Sheed and Ward, 1969).

* * *

To a large extent this chapter is an attempt to express and synthesise in reasonably simple language Rahner's thoughts as expressed particularly in the above writings.

Regarding the official teaching of the Church on Jesus' awareness of his identity, Rahner has the following to say:

The Church's doctrinal pronouncements command us to hold fast to the direct vision of the Logos (i.e. *Word*) by the human soul of Jesus. They do not, however, give us any theological instructions as to what precise concept of this vision of God we must hold. It is perfectly permissible to say that this unsystematic, global basic condition of sonship and of direct presence to the Logos includes implicit knowledge of everything connected with the mission and soteriological task of

Our Lord. In this way one will also do full justice to the marginal and incidental declarations of the Church's *magisterium* which point in this direction, without having to suppose for this reason that Jesus possessed a permanent, reflex and fully-formed propositional knowledge of everything after the manner of an encyclopedia or of a huge, actually completed world-history ('Dogmatic Reflections on the Knowledge and Self-Consciousness of Christ', *loc cit* p 213-214, first italicised word mine).

For the quotation from E. Schillebeeckx see *art cit, loc cit* , p 49:
The absolute mystery of God reverberates upon and flows into the very being of man ... Reference to the absolute mystery of God belongs to the very being of man. Being present to oneself, self-awareness is therefore in the last analysis religious, is inescapably a religious act. To stand before oneself is to stand before God (See also *God and Man*, especially pp 214f).
This idea is basic to the theology of Karl Rahner. See, for example, 'History of the World and Salvation History', *loc cit*; 'The Need for 'A Short Formula' of Christian Faith', *loc cit*, pp 122f; 'On The Theology of the Incarnation', *loc cit*, pp 107f; *Foundations of Christian Faith* , especially I to V.

Our experience of God is described as an experience of an 'horizon' by Karl Rahner; see especially 'History of the World and Salvation History', *loc cit*, pp 102f; 'The Need for 'A Short Formula' of Christian Faith', *loc cit*, p 122.

Brian O. McDermott expresses Rahner's theology of the consciousness of Christ in Trinitarian terms as follows:
I would try to express Rahner's point in Trinitarian terms this way. In Christ's human consciousness, God the Father is 'known' in a nonobjectifying way as the ultimate source of his life and love, 'known' as the divine Thou in Christ's life, to whom he was completely dedicated. In his human consciousness, the divine Word is 'known' in a nonobjectifying way as the divine relation to the Father grounding Christ's human life and human loves. And in his human consciousness, the Holy Spirit is `known', again in a nonobjectifying way, as the divine gift who unites the Father and the Son in the radiance and love of the gift. In this unitary and threefold consciousness, the humanity of Christ relates to God as Mystery more than we allow God to be Mystery for us. Mystery here is not a term for deficiency but for richness and abundance, abundance that Christ's finite human consciousness cannot encompass but 'knows' to the degree that he lets God encompass him through the course of his life into the darkness and seeming abandonment of death (*op cit*, pp.204-5. Concerning the Trinitarian aspect of Rahner's account of the consciousness of Jesus, see also Walter Kasper's note, *op cit*, p 271, note 60).

NOTES TO CHAPTER SEVEN

Further reading:

Boff, Leonardo, *Jesus Christ Liberator*, (London: S.P.C.K., 1980).

Brown, Raymond E., *The Virginal Conception and the Bodily Resurrection of Jesus*; (New York: Paulist Press, 1973);

   The Birth of the Messiah (New York: Doubleday, 1979);

   Responses to 101 Questions on the Bible (New York: Paulist Press, 1990).

Fitzmyer, Joseph A., *A Christological Catechism* (New York: Paulist Press, 1991).

Kung, Hans, *Credo: The Apostles's Creed Explained For Today* (London: SCM, 1993).

Mackey, James P., *Jesus the Man and the Myth* (London: SCM, 1979).

McDermott, Brian O., *Word Become Flesh: Dimensions of Christology* (Collegeville, Minnesota, A Michael Glazier Book, Liturgical Press, 1993).

O'Collins, Gerald, *Interpreting Jesus* (London: Chapman, 1983).

Ratzinger, Joseph, *Introduction to Christianity* (London: Burns & Oates, 1969;

   Daughter Zion (San Francisco: Ignatius Press, 1983).

Rahner, Karl, *Mary Mother of the Lord* (Wheathamsptead, Hertfordshire: Anthony Clarke, 1963;

   'Mary's Virginity' in *Theological Investigations*, vol 19 (London: Darton, Longman & Todd, 1983);

   'Reflections on the Theology of Renunciation' in *Theological Investigations*, vol 3 (London: Darton, Longman & Todd, 1967).

Schillebeeckx, Edward, *Jesus: An Experiment in Christology* (London: Collins, 1979).

Vawter, Bruce, *This Man Jesus* (London: Geoffrey Chapman, 1975).

* * *

Joseph Ratzinger's statement about Jesus not being 'half God, half man' is made in *Introduction to Christianity*, p 208.

The point that God is not the biological father of Jesus is, as we might expect, one which is commonly made by the theologians listed above. Consequently, we find theologians generally saying that the point of the virginal conception is not so as to enable God to be the Father of Jesus. So, Karl Rahner says:

> If, therefore, the Son of God willed to become man, without having an earthly father, that is not because he has a father in heaven, but for some other reason (*Mary Mother of the Lord*, p 67; see also Raymond E. Brown, *The Virginal Conception and Bodily Resurrection* of Jesus, p 42).

Gerald O'Collins says:

> Since medieval times Catholic theology has been clear that the divinity of Jesus Christ would not have been affected if he had been Joseph's son. In theory he could have been the product of normal human marriage and intercourse, without ceasing to be Son of God. Divine and

human generation are on different levels and not mutually exclusive (*op cit*, p. 196).

Joseph Ratzinger, writing again in 1977 on the subject of the virginal conception in his book *Daughter Zion*, refers to his 1968 statement that:

> ... the doctrine of Jesus' divinity would not be affected if Jesus had been the product of a normal human marriage (*op cit*, 208, see full quotation in the main text).

This is a statement which, in the meantime, Hans Urs von Balthasar had criticised on the grounds that Jesus could hardly have related as 'son' to two fathers:

> Could this man, who stood in such a unique relation to the 'Father in heaven' ... simultaneously owe his existence to another father? To put it bluntly, could he have two fathers, which would humanly have caused him to be indebted to two fathers? ... Must not Jesus' exclusive relationship to his heavenly father have offended deeply the carpenter Joseph, if he had been his natural parent? ... (quoted by Joseph Ratzinger in *Daughter Zion*, pp 49-50; see also p 51, note 11).

(Do some of the phrases Von Balthasar uses here – for example, about Jesus simultaneously owing his existence 'to another father' and being 'indebted to two fathers' – risk giving the impression that he sees the divine 'fatherhood' as being on the same level as human fatherhood? In any case, his point, it seems to me, is one which, *mutatis mutandis*, might be made of anyone who can address God as 'Father', for example, in the Lord's prayer.)

Joseph Ratzinger takes von Balthasar's point and the criticism contained in it (*loc cit*, note 11). But he does not withdraw his earlier statement; he only emphasises, as he says, its 'limits'. He explains that what he meant to say was that God is not the biological father of Jesus and that, since this is not what faith means by the divine Fatherhood, it is not for this reason that Jesus had no human father – this is also the context in which I have quoted his statement in the main text. However, he goes on to point out that this is not to imply that there is not a 'correspondence' between Jesus' Sonship of the Father and 'the earthly fatherlessness of the man Jesus'. And he describes this 'correspondence' not only as 'deep', but as 'indissoluble' (*Daughter Zion*, p 51, note 11) and says:

> To be born without an earthly father has an inner necessity for him who alone might say to God 'my Father', who was Son from the depth of his being as man, Son of this Father ... The virgin birth is the necessary origin of him who is the Son ... (pp 50-51).

A point which I find difficult to understand is how, in view of this latter statement, the 1968 statement can be said only to have 'limits'. If there is question of a 'correspondence' between two things which really is 'indissoluble', and if the two things are linked by what really is 'an inner necessity', how could one exist without the other and how, in that case, could it be true that 'the doctrine of Jesus' divinity would not be affected if Jesus had been the product of a normal human marriage' (*Introduction to Christianity*, p 208)? If the virginal conception is 'the necessary origin of him who is the Son … ' how could he be Son without this virginal conception? Ratzinger does not explain this. Obviously, however, he does not see any contradiction between his two statements and, so, does not wish to withdraw the earlier one.

For Raymond E. Brown's point about the scriptural basis for the Sonship of Jesus not being confined to the infancy stories, see *The Virginal Conception and the Bodily Resurrection of Jesus*, p 40.

Brown makes the point about Mary's own choice being for the married state, *op cit*, p 42.

Bishop Paulo Eduardo Andrade Ponte's remarks are quoted by Leonardo Boff, *op cit*, p 168.

NOTES TO CHAPTER EIGHT

Further reading:

Brown, Raymond E., 'Aspects of New Testament Thought: Christology' in *The New Jerome Biblical Commentary* (London: Chapman, 1990);
  'Does the New Testament Call Jesus God?' in *Jesus God and Man*,(London: Geoffrey Chapman, 1968).

Fitzmyer, Joseph A., 'Pauline Theology' in *The New Jerome Biblical Commentary* (London: Chapman, 1990).

Hick, John, *Christianity at the Centre*, (London: SCM, 1968).

Knox, John, *The Humanity and Divinity of Christ* (Cambridge: CUP, 1967).

Macquarrie, John, *Principles of Christian Theology* (London: SCM, revised edition, 1977).

Nolan, Brian M., 'Nature' in *The New Dictionary of Theology*, ed J. A. Komonchak and others (Dublin: Gill and Macmillan, 1987).

Rahner, Karl, *Foundations of Christian Faith* (London: Darton, Longman & Todd, 1978);
  'Current Problems in Christology' and 'Theos in the New Testament' in *Theological Investigations*, vol 1, (London: Darton, Longman & Todd, 1961);
  'Incarnation' and 'Jesus Christ' in *Sacramentum Mundi*, vol 3, ed Karl Rahner, (London: Burns Oates, 1969).

Wright, G.E., *God Who Acts: Theology as Recital* (London: SCM, 1966).

* * *

The point about the meaning of 'is' in simple statements about Jesus is one which Karl Rahner makes frequently. So, he says, for example:

  The Christological 'is'-statements – 'one and the same ' is God and man – are exposed to the perpetual risk of false interpretation because of their resemblance to the 'is'-statements of everyday life. The identity which the form of words suggests, but which is not really meant at all, is not excluded clearly and radically enough by the explanation, which inevitably comes second, and in any case because secondary is soon forgotten. That is not an argument against the justification and abiding validity of these Christological 'is'-statements. But it is obvious that they involve the danger of a Monophysite and therefore mythological misunderstanding. If, for instance, someone says today, 'After all I cannot believe that a man is God, that God has become a man', the immediate correct Christian reaction to such a statement would not be to think that a fundamental Christian dogma has been rejected. It would be to answer that the rejected statement and the construction apparently put upon it do not in fact correspond to its real Christian meaning. The true Incarnation of the Logos is indeed a mystery which calls for the act of faith, but it must not be encumbered with mythological misunderstandings ... (*Sacramentum Mundi*, vol 3, p 196; see also, Rahner, *Foundations of Christian Faith*, pp 290ff).

For an account of the Church's struggles to express accurately the relationship between the human and divine in Jesus, see the references in the notes to Chapter One.

For Rahner's position regarding the implications of the rejection of monothelitism for understanding what Chalcedon meant by of 'nature' (*physis*), see especially 'Current Problems in Christology', *loc cit*, and the articles 'Incarnation' and 'Jesus Christ' in *Sacramentum Mundi*, vol 3. With regard to the position of theologians generally, Brian M Nolan says:

Whether it is a question of the nature of the triune God, of the Son made flesh, or of other humans, contemporary theologians no longer present such a nature in static, atemporal or essentialist dress. Each of them is depicted as dynamic and open to relationships, and is shot through with the befriending graciousness of our God (*art cit, loc cit*, p 712).

My preliminary statement of the Christian position regarding Jesus is to be clearly distinguished from Adoptianism. This latter, as the reader who is familiar with the christological controversies of the early centuries will know, was an early understanding of Jesus which saw him simply as a human being who, because of his fidelity and the general moral excellence of his life, was adopted by God as Son (see Richardson, *op cit*, pp 46f, and Young, *op cit*, pp. 37f). As will become clear in the following chapters, Jesus was not a human being who was subsequently united to the Word of God, but was uttered by God as the Word Incarnate and, so, was *constituted in being* as God's 'Word Incarnate' – in Augustine's phrase '*ipsa assumptione creatur*'.

For the use of the word 'God' in the New Testament, see Karl Rahner, 'Theos in the New Testament', *loc cit*; Raymond E. Brown, 'Does the New Testament Call Jesus God?', *loc cit*; also *Responses*, pp 97f; Joseph A. Fitzmyer, *A Christological Catechism*, pp 98-99.

John Macquarrie gives his reasons for preferring to speak of Jesus as being 'definitive' rather than simply 'unique' in God's plan in *op cit*, pp 303f, especially 304-5.

The point about Jesus having been first spoken of as one in whom God was active in a 'unique and decisive way', see G. Wright, *op cit*, pp 33ff; John Hick, *op cit*, pp 11ff. *Cf* also John Knox, *op cit*, pp 56ff; 113ff. Regarding the christology of the New Testament, Raymond E. Brown says:

> NT christology was primarily functional, indicating what role Jesus played in effecting God's salvation of human beings (*pro nobis*); but in so doing, it reflects much about what Jesus was in himself (*in se*) ...
> ('Aspects of New Testament Thought: Christology', *loc cit*, p 1359 (81: 24).

Regarding Paul's christology, Joseph A. Fitzmyer says: '... one must insist on its functional character' ('Pauline Theology', *loc cit*, p 1388 (82: 28).

For the phrase 'high-water mark of God's providential activity' see John Macquarrie, *op cit*, p 314.

NOTES TO CHAPTER NINE

Further Reading:

Lane, Dermot A., *Christ at the Centre: Selected Issues in Christology* (Dublin: Veritas Publications, 1990).

Macquarrie, John, *Principles of Christian Theology* (London: SCM, revised edition, 1977).

McDermott, Brian O., *Word Become Flesh: Dimensions of Christology* (Collegeville, Minnesota, Liturgical Press, 1993).

O'Collins, Gerald, *Interpreting Jesus* (London: Geoffrey Chapman, 1983).

O'Donnell, John J., *The Mystery of the Triune God* (London: Sheed & Ward, A Heythrop Monograph, 1987).

Rahner, Karl, 'Christology Within An Evolutionary View of the World' in *Theological Investigations*, vol 5 (London: Darton, Longman & Todd, 1966).

'On the Theology of the Incarnation' and 'The Theology of Symbol' in *Theological Investigations*, vol 4 (London: Darton, Longman & Todd, 1966).

Robinson, John A., *Honest To God* (London: SCM, 1963).

***

The quotation from John A. Robinson is from *op cit*, p 71.

As this book tries to explain rather than to justify the Christian understanding of the relation between Jesus and God, the Christian view regarding the universal significance of Christ, or his implications for other religions, is not discussed here. For a brief account of the views of Catholic theologians on this matter, together with a bibliography, see Brian O. McDermott, *op cit*, pp 281ff; also Gerald O'Collins, *op cit*, 202ff.

NOTES TO CHAPTER TEN

Further Reading:

Lane, Dermot A., *Christ at the Centre* (Dublin: Veritas, 1990).

Macquarrie, John, *Principles of Christian Theology* (London: SCM, revised edition, 1977).

McDermott, Brian O., *Word Become Flesh* (Collegeville, Minnesota: Liturgical Press, 1993).

Rahner, Karl, 'On the Theology of the Incarnation' in *Theological Investigations*, vol 4 (London: Darton, Longman & Todd, 1966);
'Christology Within An Evolutionary View of the World' in *Theological Investigations*, vol 5, (London: Darton, Longman and Todd, 1966);
'Current Problems in Christology' in *Theological Investigations*, vol 1 (London: Darton, Longman & Todd, 1965);
'Jesus Christ' and 'Incarnation' in *Sacramentum Mundi*, vol 3, ed Karl Rahner (London: Burns & Oates, 1969).

Sölle, Dorothy, *Christ The Representative: An Essay in Theology after the 'Death of God'*, (London: SCM, 1967).

* * *

The quotation from Karl Rahner about the uniqueness of the unity between Jesus and God is from *Sacramentum Mundi*, vol 3, p 196.

The point that, through the Incarnation, the history of the cosmos is God's own history is made by Karl Rahner in, for example, 'Current Problems in Christology', *loc cit*, p 165.

Regarding the cosmic dimension of Christ, see also Dermot Lane, *Christ at the Centre*, pp 142f; Brian O. McDermott, *op cit*, pp 281f; Gerald O'Collins, *op cit*, pp 202f.

The quotation from Pope John Paul II is from *Dominum et Vivificatum* (Vatican City, 1986), no 50.

NOTES TO CHAPTER ELEVEN

Further Reading:

Callahan, Daniel (ed), *God, Jesus, and Spirit* (London: Geoffrey Chapman, 1969).

de Mello, Anthony, *The Song of the Bird* (Gujarat, India, Anand, 6th edition, 1985).

Macquarrie, John, *Principles of Christian Theology* (London: SCM, revised edition, 1977).

Rahner, Karl, 'Grace' in *Sacramentum Mundi*, vol 2 (London: Burns and Oates, 1968);

'Incarnation' and 'Jesus Christ' in *Sacramentum Mundi*, vol 3 (London: Burns and Oates, 1968);

'Current Problems in Christology' in *Theological Investigations*, vol 1 (London: Darton, Longman & Todd, 1965);

'Christ Within an Evolutionary View of the World' in *Theological Investigations*, vol 5 (London: Darton, Longman & Todd, 1966);

'Why Does God Allow Us to Suffer?' in *Theological Investigations*, vol 19 (London: Darton, Longman & Todd, 1984).

Schoonenber, Piet, *The Christ* (New York: Herder and Herder, 1971).

* * *

On the problem of evil and suffering, see Karl Rahner, 'Why Does God Allow Us to Suffer?', *loc cit*; John Macquarrie, *op cit*, pp 22ff, especially p 26.

EPILOGUE: REFERENCES

Brian Friel reference, *Wonderful Tennessee*, (Oldcastle, Ireland: Gallery Books, 1993).

For Angela's game, see pp 65f.

For Frank's thoughts about the monks and the book 'without words', see pp 52f.

For the description of the pier, see stage directions before the beginning of the play.

NOTES TO APPENDIX ONE

Further reading:

Inspiration:

Brown, R. E., *Responses to 101 Questions On the Bible* (New York: Paulist Press, 1990), pp 54f.

Collins, Raymond F., 'Inspiration' in *The New Jerome Biblical Commentary*, ed. Raymond E. Brown and others (London: Geoffrey Chapman, 1990), 65: 1-72.

Fitzmyer, J. A., *A Christological Catechism*, (New York: Paulist Press, 1990), pp 11f.

Harrington, W., *The Jesus Story*, (Dublin: Columba Press, 1991), pp 11-14.

Lane, D., *The Reality of Jesus*, (Dublin: Veritas, 1975), pp 32f.

Meier, John P., 'Jesus' in *The New Jerome Biblical Commentary* (London: Chapman, 1990).

A Marginal Jew: Rethinking the Historical Jesus (London: Geoffrey Chapman, 1993.)

Rahner, Karl, *Inspiration in the Bible* (New York: Herder and Herder, revised edition, 1964).

Jesus as he lived in history:
Sanders, E. P., *The Historical Figure of Jesus* (London: Allen Lane/Penguin, 1993).
Schmidt, Peter, *How to Read the Gospels: Historicity and truth in the Gospels and Acts*, trans. C. Vanhove-Romanik (Maynooth, Ireland, St Pauls, 1993).

NOTES TO APPENDIX TWO

Further reading:
Boff, Leonardo, *Jesus Christ Liberator* , (London: S.P.C.K., 1980).
Brown, Raymond E., *The Virginal Conception and the Bodily Resurrection of Jesus*; (New York: Paulist Press, 1973);
  The Birth of the Messiah (New York: Doubleday, 1979);
  Responses to 101 Questions on the Bible (New York: Paulist Press, 1990).
Fitzmyer, Joseph A., *A Christological Catechism* (New York: Paulist Press, 1991).
Kung, Hans, *Credo: The Apostles's Creed Explained For Today* (London: SCM, 1993).
Mackey, James P., *Jesus the Man and the Myth* (London: SCM, 1979).
McDermott, Brian O., *Word Become Flesh: Dimensions of Christology* (Collegeville, Minnesota, A Michael Glazier Book, Liturgical Press, 1993).
O'Collins, Gerald, *Interpreting Jesus* (London: Chapman, 1983).
Ratzinger, Joseph, *Introduction to Christianity* (London: Burns & Oates, 1969;
  Daughter Zion (San Francisco: Ignatius Press, 1983).
Rahner, Karl, *Mary Mother of the Lord* (Wheathamsptead, Hertfordshire: Anthony Clarke, 1963;
  'Mary's Virginity' in *Theological Investigations*, vol 19 (London: Darton, Longman & Todd, 1983);
  'Reflections on the Theology of Renunciation' in *Theological Investigations*, vol 3 (London: Darton, Longman & Todd, 1967).
Schillebeeckx, Edward, *Jesus: An Experiment in Christology* (London: Collins, 1979).
Vawter, Bruce, *This Man Jesus* (London: Geoffrey Chapman, 1975).

* * *

In his *The Birth of the Messiah*, a major work of scholarship, Raymond E. Brown, has this to say about the scriptural evidence for the historicity of the virginal conception of Jesus:

In my book on the virginal conception, written before I did this commentary, I came to the conclusion that the scientifically controllable biblical evidence leaves the question of the historicity of the virginal conception unresolved. The resurvey of the evidence necessitated by the commentary (i.e. *The Birth of the Messiah*) leaves me even more convinced of that. To believers who have never studied the problems critically before, this conclusion may seem radical. To many scholars who

have long since dismissed the virginal conception as theological dram-
atization, this conclusion may seem retrogressively conservative.
(And I would shock them more by affirming that I think that it is easier
to explain the NT evidence by positing historical basis than by positing pure theological creation.) I hope only that I have presented the
evidence accurately enough to have induced the readers to further
study and to their own conclusions about the evidence (*The Birth of the
Messiah*, pp 527-8 *sic*).

One of the passages in which Brown states his own position is worth
quoting here:

> ... I accept the virginal conception, but I do so primarily because of
> Church teaching on that subject. ... I contend that the biblical evidence
> does not contradict the historicity of the virginal conception. Yet I ad-
> mit that one cannot prove the virginal conception on the basis of bibli-
> cal evidence, and that is why I would appeal to Church doctrine as
> solving the ambiguities left from the biblical accounts (*Responses to 101
> Questions on the Bible*, p 89).

Joseph A. Fitzmyer says:

> In sum, one has to recognize that the New Testament data about this
> question are not unambiguous; they do not necessarily support the
> claim that this belief was a matter of 'the constant teaching of the
> Church from the beginning' (M. Schmaus, 'Mariology', *Sacramentum
> Mundi*, ...). The data suggest rather than this belief became part of the
> developing christology of the early church, within New Testament
> times, to be sure, but they are not part of the earliest tradition (*op cit*, p
> 35).

The phrase *God of Surprises* is the title of a book by Gerard W. Hughes
(London: Darton, Longman, Todd, Ltd., 1985).

NOTES TO APPENDIX THREE

Further Reading:

Grillmeier, Aloys, *Christ in Christian Tradition* (London & Oxford: Mow-
    brays, revised edition, 1975).

Kasper, Walter, *Jesus the Christ* (London: Burns & Oates, 1976).

McDermott, Brian O., *Word Become Flesh: Dimensions of Christology* (Col-
    legeville, Minnesota, Liturgical Press, 1993.

Nolan, Brian M., 'Hypostasis', 'Person, Divine', 'Nature' in *The New Dict-
    ionary of Theology*, ed J. A. Komonchak, (Dublin: Gill and Macmillan,
    1987).

O'Collins, Gerald, *Interpreting Jesus* (London: Geoffrey Chapman, 1983).

Rahner, Karl 'Current Problems in Christology' in *Theological Investiga-
    tions*, vol 1 (London: Darton, Longman & Todd, 1961).

Rahner, Karl, - Vorgrimler, Herbert, *Concise Theological Dictionary* (London: Burns & Oates, second edition, 1983).

For the terms 'hypostatic union', 'person' etc, see Walter Kasper, *op cit*, pp 230ff; Gerald O'Collins, *op cit*, pp 170ff; Karl Rahner, *art cit*, especially pp 155ff; Brian M. Nolan, *art cit*, *loc cit*, pp 500f; Brian O McDermott, *op cit*, Chapter 7, especially pp 272f.

Regarding Jesus being a distinct 'psychological' subject from the Word of God, see Rahner's comment on the significance of the 'verbally slight but theologically important' last minute omission from the text of Pope Pius XII's encyclical on Chalcedon, *Sempiternus Rex*, in 1951, *art cit*, pp 159ff. See also Walter Kasper, *op cit*; Gerald O'Collins, *op cit*, 190.

The passage quoted from the Council of Ephesus is translated by Aloys Grillmeier, *op cit*, p 486.

Index of Subjects